Bloom's

GUIDES

Homer's
The Iliad

1984
The Adventures of Huckleberry Finn
All the Pretty Horses
Beloved
Brave New World
The Chosen
The Crucible
Cry, the Beloved Country
Death of a Salesman
The Grapes of Wrath
Great Expectations
Hamlet
The Handmaid's Tale
The House on Mango Street
I Know Why the Caged Bird Sings
The Iliad
Lord of the Flies
Macbeth
Maggie: A Girl of the Streets
The Member of the Wedding
Pride and Prejudice
Ragtime
Romeo and Juliet
The Scarlet Letter
Snow Falling on Cedars
A Streetcar Named Desire
The Things They Carried
To Kill a Mockingbird

Bloom's
GUIDES

Homer's
The Iliad

Edited & with an Introduction
by Harold Bloom

CHELSEA HOUSE
P U B L I S H E R S
A Haights Cross Communications Company ®

Philadelphia

A Haights Cross Communications ⟍ Company ®

www.chelseahouse.com

Contributing editor: Pamela Loos
Cover design by Takeshi Takahashi
Layout by EJB Publishing Services

Introduction © 2005 by Harold Bloom.

Printed and bound in the United States of America.

First Printing
1 3 5 7 9 8 6 4 2

Library of Congress Cataloguing-in-Publication Data
The Iliad / Harold Bloom [editor].
    p. cm. — (Bloom's guides)
    Includes bibliographical references and index.
    ISBN 0-7910-8240-7 (alk. paper)
    1. Homer. Iliad—Examinations—Study guides. 2. Epic poetry,
Greek—Examinations—Study guides. 3. Achilles (Greek mythology) in
literature. 4. Trojan War—Literature and the war. I. Bloom, Harold.
II. Series.
    PA4037.I44 2004
    883'.01—dc22
                                            2004026183

Every effort has been made to trace the owners of copyrighted material and secure copyright permission. Articles appearing in this volume generally appear much as they did in their original publication with little to no editorial changes. Those interested in locating the original source will find bibliographic information in the bibliography and acknowledgments sections of this volume.

Contents

 Introduction

HAROLD BLOOM

Together with the Bible, the *Iliad* represents the foundation of Western literature, thought, and spirituality: of culture in the broadest sense. That banal truism contains the permanent split in Western consciousness: Our cognition and aesthetics are Greek, but our religion and morality—whether Christian, Moslem, Judaic—make us people of the Book, and the book is not the *Iliad*, as it was for classical culture. We are not at once very close to the *Iliad*, even when we first encounter it, and enormously estranged from it. The largest of Simone Weil's many eccentricities came when she closely associated the Gospels and the *Iliad*, while opposing to them the Hebrew Bible and Roman literature. Jesus and Achilles do not pair at all easily, and the morality of the *Iliad* is totally antithetical to that of the New Testament. This division in Western consciousness never has been healed, even by Shakespeare, whose Hamlet is far closer to King David than to Achilles or to Hector, and whose Lear sustains comparison with the Solomon of Ecclesiastes and the apocryphal Wisdom of Solomon much more readily than with Priam, or with Peleus, the wretched father of Achilles. The *Iliad* was the schoolbook of Athens, and we, all of us, are still attending the school of Athens, but we are there as aliens, barbarians not wholly at one with the thought-forms and aesthetic shapes that necessarily we must absorb if we are to be coherent beings.

The *Iliad* centers upon telling us that the highest good is victory, explicitly in war, implicitly in art and thought: indeed in every human endeavor. Homer teaches *agon*, the contest for the foremost place, a teaching we ourselves honor more readily in politics or in sport or in business or in law, than we do in the arts and in the other realms of the intellect and the spirit. Achilles, best of the Greeks, is the epitome of the agonistic. His language, as Adam Parry observed, is "a form of action," and yet he is able to hint his disillusionment with his own glory, and with nature, for denying him literal immortality. Adam Parry remarks that Achilles "asks questions that cannot be answered and makes demands that cannot be met." Homer's complexity contains Achilles' extraordinary dilemma: The hero has wearied of the *agon*, and no longer desires its spoils. But he cannot abandon a society that knows no value except the agonistic ones, and he has no language beyond that of *agon*. Hamlet, radically alienated from Elsinore, has infinite resources of language in which to exploit that alienation, even though Hamlet also has abandoned all faith in language or in the self, his own included. The epic plangency of Achilles is that he turns again to action as his form of language, and paradoxically kills out of his very hatred for mortality, including his own mortality.

The heroes of the Hebrew Bible—Abraham, Jacob, Joseph, David—have no affinities whatsoever with Achilles. Even David, the only professional warrior among them, carries on their blessing from Yahweh and so is in a position beyond tragedy, despite his many griefs that terminate in the death of his beloved son, Absalom. You can make a covenant with Yahweh and then trust in the covenant, but no one can trust Zeus. Achilles is half a god, and he says that "who trusts himself to the gods will gain their hearing," but he knows that the response to such a hearing is likely to be equivocal, and they cannot free him from war, since despite his disillusion he *is* war and nothing but war. The poetic strength of Achilles is that he is a force or a drive, even though he feels, thinks, and perceives as a man. No other purely literary figure is nearly as heroic, or as aesthetically satisfying to us, but Achilles' *otherness*, in relation to us, is now his dominant characteristic.

Biographical Sketch

Homer, the blind poet, is generally regarded as the author of the *Iliad* and the *Odyssey*, which are dated to be from the end of the eighth century or early seventh century B.C. Numerous Greek cities claim themselves as Homer's birthplace, but scholars now believe Smyrna and Chios (across the Aegean Sea from mainland Greece) to be the most logical locations. Nothing is known of Homer's life, although ancient Greeks viewed him as a wandering, poverty-stricken minstrel.

Some scholars, however, have questioned whether one person wrote the *Iliad* and the *Odyssey* and whether, in turn, each of these might have been created by more than one person. The differences in the language, social customs, and view of the gods from the *Iliad* to the *Odyssey* were what the "separatists" pointed to as proof that the works were not developed by one man. Yet for the "unitarians" and Ancient Greeks, who believed one author was responsible for both, the differences are feasible in light of the very differing subjects of the works. Similarly, the language of the two is similar, and the *Odyssey* is a sequel to the *Iliad*, with the characters from one to the other remaining constant in personality.

When in the eighteenth century it was espoused that Homer didn't, in fact, write, it was questioned how such long works could have been created. The idea was proposed that that there was a core of shorter ballad-type poems that had been composed and that these had been expanded upon over the years by collective effort or perhaps by one editor. This concept also would account for discrepancies within the works. Attempts to show, however, that the work had been created over an extended period of time proved fruitless. For example, analyzing the linguistic features proved problematic, partially because the language of the poem was one created solely for poetic use and had not ever been spoken. Similarly, analyzing the work from a historical perspective proved ineffective, since while it appeared that different sections were written at different times, the results obtained by those with a historical perspective did not match results obtained by other methods that had been used to date the sections. Archaeological examination proved equally frustrating.

The work of Milman Parry provided new information on the tradition of oral poetry and composition. He studied material comparable to Homer's work that was still surviving in Yugoslavia and suggested that discrepancies and seeming inconsistences in Homer were likely if his composing techniques had followed the centuries-old tradition of oral poetry. For example, while many had commented on Homer's use of repeated phrases, assuming they were used to fill out lines to their required number of stresses, now it was theorized that these were indeed used to fill out lines but that they were designed to help the performer. For example, if there were a few phrases available when describing Achilles, the reciter could choose one extemporaneously to fit his need for a particular line.

Over time, many scholars reverted to the earlier belief that Homer did write, and they assumed that the traditions of oral poetry were key in the final form of his work. Under this assumption then, one man could have created work that was so lengthy, complex, and subtle. It was theorized, also, that if Homer couldn't write himself, he may have dictated to scribes.

It is clear that however the poems were composed that they were done with the intent that the material would be performed. In Homer's time epics were sung or chanted to the music of a lyre by a professional reciter, called a rhapsode ("song-stitcher"). Rhapsodes memorized various pieces but also probably expanded on them or created varying personal versions. Performances would take place at public festivals; by 776 B.C. Greeks held Panathenaic games of athletic and poetic competitions (a model for the Olympic games). It has been surmised that the *Iliad* would have been sung in excerpts, since estimates state that if performed in one sitting it would require more than twenty hours of performance and that it would also be difficult to divide into sections with breaks, since the action is continuous. The idea of performing in excerpts also makes sense in light of the fact that the singers in Homer's time were familiar with memorizing works probably between one hundred and five hundred lines long, whereas Homer's works are more than thirty times this length. By the sixth century B.C., Homer's works were probably available in written format. However, they were still memorized and performed, and memorization by students was also considered a key component of education. By the fourth and fifth centuries B.C., copies were available throughout the Greek world. The *Iliad* was edited and written about by scholars in Alexandria in the fourth century B.C., who also created a standard edition. They utilized papyrus rolls, where the text was written in columns on the inside of the roll. If the rolls were too big, they could break when used for reading, so the *Iliad* probably was split into twenty-four rolls, which would account for the twenty-four books we see in our printed versions today. Later, in the second to fifth centuries A.D., parchment replaced the papyrus and folded sewn-together sections replaced rolls. The first printed edition of Homer was created in 1488 in Florence by an immigrant scholar who taught Greek in Italy. From there, numerous editions and translations have been created from the original Greek of more than 15,000 lines.

The Story Behind the Story

Was there an actual Trojan War? If so, how closely do the events in Homer's *Iliad* follow the historical event? For the Greeks, the epic was indeed history, and this perspective was not seriously questioned until the nineteenth century. But even then such skeptics were held at bay when new information was provided by the archaeologist Heinrich Schliemann, who excavated sites at Troy, Mycenae, and other locations described in the *Iliad*, and Sir Arthur Evans, who excavated at Cnossos. (See the Bernard Knox introduction in the Robert Fagles' translation of the *Iliad*.) These men found bronze armor, weapons, and objects that seemed to match Homer's descriptions in the epic. These items seemed to match the date ancient Greek scholars had assigned to the war. Additionally, in the 1950s clay tablets found at some of these excavated cities were determined to be composed of a stage of the Greek language having characteristics that closely matched some aspects of the *Iliad*'s language.

Upon closer inspection, however, the tablets were found to be daily ledgers of a bureaucratic monarchy and didn't indicate a connection to the stories in Homer's work. Names from the *Iliad* do occur on the tablets, yet, for example, a Hector is described not as a commander-in-chief or heir to Troy's throne but as a "servant of the god" who "holds a lease." Similarly, the work at the site of Hissarlik, which was decided to be the probable site of Homer's Troy, provided no clear explanation of how the city met its end. It is one of many in the Near East that were destroyed during the late Bronze Age, and its destruction may have been from an earthquake, not necessarily from war.

Still, some scholars have placed the Trojan War in a historical context. They see the Achaeans from the *Iliad* as the Mycenaeans, who lived in the city of Mycenae on mainland Greece, were rich, and were so powerful that from approximately 1600 B.C. to 1150 B.C. they controlled the area around the Aegean Sea. These scholars believe that the *Iliad*'s war may refer to a raid in the thirteenth century B.C., when the Mycenaean rulers attacked Troy. They point to Schliemann's discoveries as evidence, since he found appropriate weapons and other artifacts, and also found that the city had a violent end. Regardless of its basis in truth, the *Iliad* has had an enormous impact on Western literature. Its form alone set a definition for epic form. Specifically, the work opens with the narrator's request that a goddess provide inspiration for his relating the tale. He starts at a key moment in the whole, not necessarily at what would be construed as the beginning, and adds information on the past and future as the narrative progresses.

Additionally, the key figures in his work have certain qualities and beliefs. For example, they have powers that are beyond the usual mortal's; they have direct interaction with gods and goddesses, with some even having been born of an immortal; and they act for their own glory or fame. Finally, Homer's poetry also shows the use of repeated phrases or epithets in his descriptions. Detailed and sometimes lengthy similes also are common. At times these similes intensify the moment or serve as a great contrast to it. Often they involve nature, seemingly a reminder that the world naturally is composed of many positive and negative facets.

"Homer was regarded with reverence by most Greeks, as the source (with Hesiod) of their knowledge of the gods, the formulator of the heroic code of conduct, a touchstone of wise behaviour; and he was constantly quoted," according to the *Oxford Companion to Classical Literature*. Plato described him as "unequalled in diction and thought." Prominent writers and thinkers have translated his work, men such as Thomas Hobbes in the seventeenth century, Alexander Pope in the eighteenth century, and William Cullen Bryant in the nineteenth century, for example. Also, translations have been written about by equally key writers. For example, Matthew Arnold wrote an essay on translating Homer, and John Keats was inspired to write the poem "On First Looking into Chapman's Homer."

Homer's work also served as inspiration for some venerated

works of literature. Virgil wrote his epic the *Aeneid*, John Milton wrote *Paradise Lost*, and James Joyce wrote his modern novel *Ulysses*, which took Odysseus's trek in the *Odyssey* and condensed it into one day in the life of a representative modern man.

List of Characters

GREEKS (Achaeans, Argives, and Danaans)

Achilles is the son of the sea-nymph goddess Thetis and the human Peleus; he is prince of the Myrmidons of Phthia in Tessaly. The central character of the *Iliad*, Achilles is the Greeks' greatest warrior but flawed to such an extent that he allows his fellow Greek armies to suffer great losses as they fight the Trojans. His personality draws readers' attention to the destructiveness of anger and stubborness and the role of the hero. Achilles receives favors from the gods yet also knows his fate is tragic and often thinks about it, drawing attention to the fact that knowing one's fate can prove a horrid albatross.

Agamemnon is the commander in the battle against Troy, is King of Mycenae, and also leader of the Argos army. He serves as a foil to Achilles and example of a poor leader. He is stubborn as well, is accused of selfishness, and usually relies on others for battle plans. He is the older brother of Menelaus, and they are each often called Atrides, meaning "son of Atreus."

Little Ajax, also called Ajax, Oilean Ajax (since he is the son of Oileus), or Locrian Ajax to distinguish him from the greater hero Ajax, son of Telamon. Little Ajax is leader of the men from Locris. Oilean Ajax is a great warrior himself yet flawed by insolence and becomes the object of a god's joke.

Great Ajax, also called Ajax or Telamonian Ajax (since he is the son of Telamon), is leader of the men from Salamis and is often referred to as second only to Achilles. He is known for his brute power and courage, with one of his greatest moments being when he fends off Trojans ready to set fire to the Greek ships. Greatly admired yet not one to speak much, he gives the shortest plea when a contingent tries to convince Achilles to fight and it is direct and realistic.

Antilochus is the son of Nestor and, along with his father and brother, leads the contingent from Pylos. He is a young warrior who is brave and dynamic in the war and active in the funeral games for Patroclus. He is chosen to bring the news of Patroclus' death to Achilles, showing he is trusted and respected.

Automedon is the squire of Achilles and driver of Achilles' immortal horses. He drives for Patroclus when Achilles sends him into war.

Calchas is the chief prophet for the Achaean warriors. His very existence with the men and the fact that he is consulted and decisions are made based on his words shows the great value the characters place on his ability to tell the future.

Diomedes is son of Tydeus and leader with Sthenelus of the armies from Argos and Tiryns. He is a great warrior, ever courageous and ruthless (to the point of killing many men in their sleep). He is the first man in the text to receive great help from the gods and to have one of the epic's books devoted to his superhuman fighting. He is also smart enough to be trusted with a special mission.

Epeius is known as the great boxing champion yet also is shown as being concerned about his opponent.

Eumelus is leader of the Thessalian contingent from Pherae. Known for his chariot-driving abilities, he competes in the chariot race at the funeral games. He serves as an example of what happens when the gods favor others. He immediately forges far ahead of the others in the race but loses because of a god's intervention.

Euryalus is one of the leaders of the Argos, under Diomedes.

He exemplifies the idea of courage and foolishness as sometimes being closely related when he takes on boxing with the champion Epeius and quickly is knocked out.

Eurybates is the principal herald or official messenger of Agamemnon and the Greek forces.

Helen is the daughter of Zeus, originally married to Menelaus, who was seduced by Paris and brought to Troy. Her leaving is the cause of the war. She has great beauty, which can be seen as a curse, since in the *Iliad* the few times she speaks she describes how guilty she feels and even that she wishes she had died before meeting Paris.

Idomeneus is the leader of the contingent from Crete. He is one of the ablest captains and a strong fighter.

Leonteus leads the Lapith army along with Polypoetes. Both are key in keeping the Trojans from the Greek ships.

Machaon, along with his brother Podalirius, leads the Tessalian men. He is the son of a famous physician, and he and his brother provide the key medical needs for the Greek soldiers. The fact that little and rudimentary medical help is available for so many men makes the fighters even more impressive figures to the modern reader.

Menelaus had been the husband of Helen, who was seduced by Paris and brought to Troy. Menelaus is also the younger brother of Agamemnon and the son of Atreus. He leads the Lacedaemonian men. He is a great fighter and also shows appreciation for others.

Menestheus is the leader of the Athenian men.

Meriones is second in command under Idomeneus of the Cretan forces.

Nestor leads, with his two sons Antilochus and Thrasymedes, the contingent from Pylos. He is the oldest of the Achaean chiefs fighting at Troy and frequently provides sage counsel. He is greatly respected. This character shows that while old age has its physical drawbacks it also can have the advantage of wisdom.

Odysseus is leader of the contingent from the island of Ithaca. He is a key fighter and man with intelligence, common sense, and tact. He is greatly respected, and when a contingent is sent to try to convince Achilles to join the fight, he is the first to speak and tries various methods of persuasion. He also goes on the spying mission with Diomedes. He is the hero of Homer's *Odyssey*.

Patroclus is a Greek fighter in the Myrmidon group and Achilles' squire and close friend, even while seeing Achilles' flaws. He stands in contrast to Achilles when he helps a wounded man and stays to care for him, while for most of the epic Achilles refuses to fight to help save Argives. Patroclus becomes a pivotal figure when he goes to war in Achilles' armor, fights bravely and with great success, but does not heed Achilles' warning about returning before the fighting moves to Troy's gates. Patroclus has empathy, is brave, and an example of what happens when advice is not followed, despite good intentions.

Phoenix is an older fighter with the Myrmidons; Achilles' father made him king of the Dolopians. He is a friend and tutor of Achilles. As part of the contingent that tries to convince Achilles to join the battle, he bursts into tears and makes an impassioned personal plea. From his speech we learn something of Achilles' early personal life, reminding us he had once been a young boy, not so different from many.

Podalirius leads, with his brother Machaon, the Thessalian men. He is a fighter and also known for his medical skills.

Polypoetes leads, with Leonteus, the Lapith contingent. He and his brother are key in keeping the Trojans from destroying the Greek ships.

Sthenelus is the friend and squire to Diomedes.

Talthybius is the chief herald or messenger for Agamemnon and the Greeks.

Teucer is the illegitimate half-brother of Telamonian Ajax. He is the Greeks' greatest bowman.

Thersites is an unruly and outspoken soldier.

Tlepolemus is son of the great hero Heracles and leader of the contingent from Rhodes.

TROJANS (Dardanians) AND THEIR ALLIES

Aeneas is son of the goddess Aphrodite and is second in command to Hector and Hector's third cousin. Achilles taunts him and questions whether he wants to be king, and earlier Poseidon suggests that this may happen.

Andromache is Hector's wife, mother of their son Scamandrius (also called Astyanax, "city lord," since Hector is seen as the city's protector), and daughter of King Thebe-under-Placus. Her presence allows a look at Hector's personal life. She is a reminder of how his actions have repercussions for the city and those who love him, and also a reminder of the great losses the Trojans have already suffered, since her birth family has been killed by Achilles.

Antenor is married to the priestess of Athena, Theano, and father of many killed by the Argives. He advises that the Trojans return Helen.

Astyanax is the baby son of Hector and Andromache. His given name is Scamandrius, but he is called Astyanax ("city lord") because the Trojans see his father as their protector.

Briseis is the woman Achilles took after he sacked the town of Lyrnessus. Achilles says he loves her. However, Agamemnon takes her from Achilles, provoking Achilles to say he will not fight, which results in the deaths of many Argives.

Cassandra is daughter of King Priam and Hecuba, and sister of Hector, Paris, Helenus, and Deïphobus.

Chryseis is the daughter of Chryses, the priest of Apollo at Chryse. She is the war prize awarded to Agamemnon, who is forced to give her back to her father and subsequently absconds Briseis, causing Achilles' wrath.

Chryses is the priest of Apollo who goes to the Achaeans to offer ransom for his daughter Chryseis.

Deïphobus is the son of Priam and Hecuba and works with his brother Hector on battle strategy.

Dolon is sent to spy on the Achaeans. He readily gives secret information to the enemy when he's captured. His behavior on the mission strongly contrasts that of Odysseus and Diomedes when they set out to spy on the Trojans.

Glaucus is second-in-command of the Lycians under his cousin Sarpedon.

Hector is the son of Priam and Hecuba, husband of Andromache, and commander-in-chief of the Trojan forces and their allies. Priam says he prizes him best of all his many sons. The Trojans see him as their protector and greatest fighter and so he is the foil to Achilles. In contrast to Achilles, we see him interact with numerous family members, accept Paris' foibles, and treat Helen with kindness. When he asks Achilles to make a pact with him that whoever is the victor will return the other's body to his army's leader, Achilles immediately scorns the idea, uncompromising yet again and lacking Hector's civility.

Hecuba is daughter of Dymas, the king of Phrygia, and consort to King Priam, with whom she has many children, including Hector. She offers Priam good advice before he leaves for the Achaean camp and stands as the prototypical woman urging caution on her husband and heroic son as well.

Helenus is the son of Priam and Hecuba. Apollo gave him the gift of prophecy.

Idaeus is the chief herald or official messenger for Priam and the Trojan army.

Pandarus is the son of King Lycaon of Lycia. He breaks the peace between the two sides an indication of how readily and easily peace can be destroyed.

Paris, also called Alexander, is the son of Priam and Hecuba, known as the cause of the war because he seduced Helen and took her to Troy, away from her Achaen husband Menelaus. He is handsome and frequently viewed unfavorably.

Polydamus is one of the ablest Trojan leaders. He contrasts with Hector, since he is cautious and level-headed in strategizing.

Priam is the king of Troy and father of Hector, Paris, Helenus, Deïphobus, Cassandra, and many others. He is an old man, who at the end of the epic manages to rouse Achilles' sympathies, appealing to him by reminding Achilles of his own old father and making Achilles appear more the human and less the hero.

Sarpedon is leader of the Lycian allies. He is a formidable fighter and famous for being Zeus' son.

GODS AND GODDESSES

Aphrodite is the goddess of love and daughter of Zeus. She fights on the Trojan side, and rescues Paris and her son Aeneas, helping also Ares, the war god.

Apollo is the son of Zeus, also called Phoebus, Phoebus Apollo, and Lord of the Silver Bow. He is the patron of bowmen, and he can bring about sudden death by disease in men. He fights for the Trojans.

Ares is the son of Zeus and Hera and the god of war. While he has promised to help on the Achaean side, he fights for the Trojans.

Artemis is the daughter of Zeus, the goddess of the chase, mistress of the bow, and protectress of wild animals. She fights for the Trojans. She, too, kills by causing disease and sudden death.

Athena, also called Pallas Athena, is the daughter of Zeus and goddess of wisdom and patroness of the arts and crafts. She is also the protectress of cities and a fighting goddess. She is a formidable force on the Achaean side.

Dione is the mother of Aphrodite by Zeus.

Hades is the god of the dead and brother of Zeus, Poseidon, and Hera.

Hebe is the goddess of youth and beauty, the daughter of Zeus and Hera. She is a handmaiden of the gods.

Hephaestus is the god of fire and patron of metalworkers, the son of Zeus and Hera and married to Charis. He has crippled legs and when called by Achilles' mother to create armor for his son, he creates masterpieces. When called by Hera, he saves Achilles from the Xanthus River.

Hera is queen of the Olympian gods, wife of Zeus, and mother of Ares, Hephaestus, and Hebe. She is the greatest support for the Achaean army, which creates tension between herself and Zeus on several occasions.

Hermes is a son of Zeus and a messenger for the gods. While he is on the Achaean side, he provides little help and is actually chosen by Zeus to guide the Trojan Priam safely to Achilles' camp.

Iris is the goddess of the rainbow and a messenger for the gods. At times she complies with human requests as well as advises recipients of her messages.

Leto is mother of the twins Apollo and Artemis and referred to as a consort of Zeus. She is for the Trojan side.

Poseidon is the god of the sea and of earthquakes and a brother of Zeus, Hades, and Hera. He usually supports the Achaeans.

Thetis is a sea goddess and was married to the mortal Peleus. She is the mother of Achilles. She aids her son as much as possible and has great sympathy for him.

Xanthus, also called Scamander, is a son of Zeus and god of one of the two key rivers by Troy. Achilles kills many men in and by the river and brazenly attempts to fight the river itself.

Zeus is the supreme Olympian god, known as the father of the gods. He is the husband of Hera and father of Athena, Aphrodite, Ares, Apollo, and others. He is the minister of destiny and so is to be neutral in the war. Still, he answers Thetis' request to help Achilles and at times also has great sympathy for the Trojans, especially Hector.

Summary and Analysis

Note: The Robert Fagles translation is used here.

"Rage—." This is the *Iliad*'s stark opening, an intense single word followed by a dash that separates it from the rest. The bearer of this rage is Achilles, the hero of the epic poem; here in the opening he and/or his rage are described as "murderous, doomed." This is an ominous start, and adding to its power is its deviance from the usual heroic tale, for we learn that the hero's intense anger is not aimed at and unleashed on his enemy. Instead it has caused death for his own people, has "cost the Achaeans countless losses,/hurling down to the House of Death so many sturdy souls." This hero who causes tragedy for his own side is one unexpected by readers in the twenty-first century, as well as having been unexpected by audiences in Ancient Greece.

Homer's contemporaries already knew of Achilles and other Greek heroes of the Trojan War, their entire story being well learned by most Greeks and a proud part of their heritage (although it is still unknown how much of the Trojan War story is true). The story's prominence has been compared to that of the bible for many today. Indeed, the narrator of the *Iliad* calls on the "Goddess," also referred to as the "Muse," to "sing" the tale through him/her, just as the writers of the New Testament were supposedly divinely inspired in telling their story.

We learn that "the will of Zeus" is also involved and that other gods partake in the human drama as well. We find that Achilles, Prince of the Myrmidons, is not just angry with Agamemnon, the King of Mycenae, but the two have been driven to fight by the gods. The dispute is sparked by Agamemnon's initial stubbornness. He refuses to return Chryseis to her old father, Chryses, who begs the whole Achaean army for her return and offers ransom. Chryses' words are the first that are directly quoted in the *Iliad*, as will be much of the text throughout, adding a great immediacy to the epic and making it similar to a dramatic work. The scholar

Eric Auerbach has explained: "With the utmost fullness, with an orderliness which even passion does not disturb, Homer's personages vent their inmost hearts in speech; what they do not say to others, they speak in their own minds, so that the reader is informed of it. Much that is terrible takes place in the Homeric poems, but it seldom takes places wordlessly...."

After Chryses begs for his daughter to no avail, the god Apollo casts a plague on the Achaeans for not giving up Chryseis. After nine days of suffering and death, Achilles draws the troops together to listen to a prophet, who explains that a god is against the Achaeans because they will not return Chryseis. At this, Agamemnon is furious yet agrees to release the woman. He insists, however, that he must then have another "prize" immediately and not only will he not be deterred by Achilles' reasoning against this but he announces that he will take the woman Achilles had been given from war booty.

The fury between the two men rises feverishly, provoking Achilles to consider killing the king. He is stopped by the goddess Athena but still lashes Agamemnon with stinging accusations and then swears he and his armies will not aid the Achaeans in their fight against the Trojans. Chryseis is returned, and Agamemnon sends his men to take Achilles' woman, Briseis. Achilles, known as the Achaeans' greatest warrior, is reduced to tears and begs his mother, the goddess Thetis, for help. He asks her to convince Zeus to help the Trojans make great gains in the war, so the Achaeans will realize what a mistake it was to disgrace Achilles and therefore not benefit from his battlefield skills. The plague is lifted from the Achaeans once Chryseis is returned, but now Zeus agrees, even at the expense of angering his wife, to turn against the Achaeans for Achilles' sake. This closes book one, the first of the epic's twenty-four books.

To put his plan into effect, Zeus first sends a dream to Agamemnon, telling the powerful king he must attack the Trojans immediately. "[G]riefs from Zeus are about to crush the men of Troy!" the dream announces and also tells Agamemnon that he and his fellow Achaens will be victorious against the Trojans. The narrator calls Agamemnon a "fool" for believing he will take Troy that day, but then, in the king's defense, points out that the man has no way of knowing Zeus' actual plan to bring great suffering to the Greeks.

Agamemnon wastes no time. He dons his armor, orders the men to gather, and calls his top military leaders together for a private meeting. He relays the dream to these men but says that before launching the attack they must follow custom and test the men by telling them they are to withdraw and return home. The commanders dash out into the amassing crowds of men:

> Rank and file
> Streamed behind and rushed like swarms of bees
> pouring out of a rocky hollow, burst on endless burst,
> bunched in clusters seething over the first spring blooms,
> dark hordes swirling into the air, this way, that way—

This powerful description is not unlike others the author uses, in that it is a vivid, extended, nature simile. The choice of bees as a metaphor for the armies is most fitting. Bees may not immediately be viewed as harmful creatures but once swarming can be quite dangerous, just as the men are a weak threat when lying low in their boats but become dangerous as they group and prepare for war. The bees' ominous-ness is reinforced by words such as "seething" and "dark" and because the bees appear unstoppable and never-ending. Also, this is similar to other descriptions in the text, in that there is a marked contrast between this swarming negative force and something positive—in this case, the first spring blooms (again another natural element) and all the beauty and delicacy they connote. Interesting also is the fact that the blooms cannot multiply without the bees, alluding to war as a seemingly natural, necessary element of life as well.

Agamemnon addresses the army throngs, explaining his reasons for ordering them to leave, among them the fact that they have been fighting here for nine years. The men are thrown into disarray, and in a state of alarm hurriedly prepare to leave. They now are compared to surging sea waves (a metaphor used again later in Book Two as well). Hera, Zeus' wife, presses the goddess Athena to interfere, for she does not want the Achaeans to leave the Trojans with the beautiful Helen. This is the first we hear of Helen, yet no further details are given about her here, although Ancient Greeks knew her part in the Trojan War stories.

Athena urges Odysseus to stop the retreat. He rallies the troops using a range of oratorial techniques. Nestor adds his own words to rouse the men to their duty. Agamemnon says he could easily beat the Trojans if he only had ten men like Nestor. He goes on to blame Zeus for entangling him in "painful struggles," and then, while still blaming Zeus, contemplates:

> Imagine—I and Achilles, wrangling over a girl,
> battling man-to-man. And I, I was the first
> to let my anger flare. Ah if the two of us
> could ever think as one, Troy could delay
> her day of death no longer, not one moment.

As we read more of the king, we will see how this self-reflection, admittance of mistake, and lack of selfishness are not a part of his regular nature. It is an unusual moment for him and one that contrasts with the descriptions of Achilles that occur later in the section.

Book two is entitled "The Great Gathering of Armies," and we see why. Not only has this been the focus of the section so far, but most of the rest of this section is spent enumerating all the leaders and where they've come from (with a word or slight description of that place or its men), as well as how many ships and men each commander leads into battle. The list of commanders and troops continues with only one interruption for nearly three hundred lines, again a reminder of the huge numbers of men. More lines do not necessarily appear for those characters we already know to be great men; nor are such men all described at the front of the list. Perhaps this is a reminder that no matter how great, all the men still must line up and march on to their possible deaths.

An interruption occurs toward the end of the list and focuses on Achilles. He is described as lying among his ships, still raging over the loss of Briseis, but we are told he "would soon rise up in all his power." Then the list continues, and when it finally is complete, Achilles is again described as raging in his ship. This time his men and even their horses are also described, waiting, finding diversions, in stark contrast to all the other marching armies.

Finally we turn to the Trojans. Zeus sends a messenger to them to warn them of the approaching men. The Trojans are ready nearly immediately. Again there is the same method of describing the list of Trojan armies as they fall into order. Yet, now, in striking contrast the list is much shorter, accounting for approximately ninety lines (rather than the almost three hundred devoted to the Achaeans).

Book three is entitled "Helen Reviews the Champions." There is some irony in this title, since, we will see, Helen is reviewing the Achaean troops, and we know from what has occurred earlier that Zeus' plan at this point is only to make the Achaeans *think* they will become ready champions. This third book has the first appearance of Helen as well. She is the intensely beautiful woman who was seduced to leave her Achaean husband, Menelaus; her child; and homeland to flee with the Trojan Paris, god-like in his beauty as well. What adds to the art of this book is that we get an unanticipated view of Helen. Here is a woman who speaks her mind and respects others; she also feels tremendously guilty and lives a life of tearful woe as a result. Also, here we see something else we wouldn't have anticipated, the Trojans' perspective on Helen. Rather than condemning her as the impetus for the bloody war that has persisted for years, the Trojans admire Helen's great looks, and the older men amongst themselves even admit that it would be best for the Trojans to give her up. But these men are old, relegated to the sidelines, their days of action behind them, and so they are not listened to.

This book opens with the great marching of the approaching Trojan and Achaean armies. From the masses springs Paris, proposing mortal combat between himself and any one of the

Achaeans rather than all-out war between the two sides. Menelaus thrills at the offer to take revenge on the man who stole his wife. When Paris recognizes the reality of what he's proposed, he shrinks back in fear and only because of intense verbal barbs from his brother Hector does he agree to go through with the fight.

The action is delayed and suspense mounts when the narrative turns away from the battlefield to the civilian Trojans in their walled city. Priam, the city's aged king, calls Helen to him as he surveys the roused Achaean troops. He asks her to name the great men he readily notices even from such a distance, envious of their might.

We are returned to the battlefield. After making ceremonial agreements and offerings to the gods, Menelaus and Paris fight. However, just when Menelaus is almost the victor, Aphrodite snatches Paris from the battlefield and rests him in his own bed, summoning Helen to have sex with him. Helen rants against the goddess and condemns and scathingly mocks Paris for his weakness. When the two are finally in bed, the narration returns to the battlefield, where the men are baffled about Paris' whereabouts. Agamemnon declares an Achaean victory.

Book four, "The Truce Erupts in War," provides a further portrayal of the gods, primarily as overly emotional and intent on getting their way. Most have chosen either the Achaeans or Trojans to fight for. Already, before any war is described in the text, we see the gods as a colossal force. They often exhibit petty human attributes and sometimes readily interfere with the mortals out of rage or love; at other times don't pay attention; at other times negotiate, threaten, or trick other gods to get their way; and at other times just give in. Many scholars have written on Homer's use of the gods. Jasper Griffin writes, "It is clear that of all the devices [of Homer] which are used to enhance the significance of action, none can be more pervasive or more profound than the existence of a pantheon of gods who are deeply concerned with the deeds and sufferings of the heroes, and who themselves constantly intervene among them.... [t]his is much more than a mere 'divine apparatus'....

[I]t stands in a peculiar and identifiable relation to real religion, and ... is of the greatest importance both for the *Iliad* and for later Greek poetry."

Zeus at the beginning of this book does consider what might be best for all mortals and immortals alike. At this point he could lead the Achaens and Trojans to truce, yet his wife convinces him against this.

Zeus sends Athena to the battlefield, and the men question, "groaning," what will happen next, pointedly showing their resignation to the gods' often unfavorable wills. The goddess provokes the Trojans' best archer to aim for Menelaus. The archer hits him, blood spurts out, and the Achaeans see this as a breaking of the truce that should be in place due to Paris' disappearance. Agamemnon greatly fears losing Menelaus, but Menelaus' wound is not so serious, and Agamemnon, now relieved, sees the Trojans approaching and realizes he must rally his men. On foot he approaches each division and uses whatever tactic he deems best—chastising, praise, inspiration, reminders of an individual's family history. This provides another opportunity for the reader or listener to be reminded of who the key Achaean leaders are, their strengths, and their personalities; this also creates further build-up to the actual war.

Then, at the near end of this fourth book, the fighting begins. First described is the horrid scene of the troops clashing. From there, we are told of the first Trojan captain killed. Names are mentioned, but most we don't know. Then Telamonian Ajax is described as killing a Trojan, and while we know Ajax is one of the Achaeans' heroes, detailed attention is given to the man he's killed, again, someone we haven't read about so far:

And Telamonian Ajax struck Anthemion's son,
the hardy stripling Simoisius, still unwed ...
His mother had borne him along the Simois' banks
when she trailed her parents down the slopes of Ida
to tend their flocks, and so they called him Simoisius.
But never would he repay his loving parents now

for the gift of rearing—his life cut short so soon,
brought down by the spear of lionhearted Ajax.

While the epic is told primarily from the Achaean view, we
see here and repeatedly throughout an attention to deaths of
characters (either Trojans or Achaeans) that were previously
unknown to us and who in a few lines, or sometimes only a few
words, become live individuals but now are killed, invoking pity
and/or a feeling of senselessness and shame.

The Achaeans' great hero Odysseus is described next,
spurred on by great fury when he sees that "his loyal comrade"
is killed trying to pull a dead man out of the battle. Odysseus'
consuming rage drives him to attack, and the Trojans, even
"glorious Hector," shrink back. Rage and revenge prove a
driving force in the text here and throughout, and it is most
fitting that just shortly after this the name of Achilles appears,
the man we had almost forgotten, who, we are reminded,
"wallows/in all his heartsick fury by the ships!"

Book four closes with no tales of glory, though, but instead:

That day ranks of Trojans, ranks of Achaean fighters
sprawled there side-by-side, facedown in the dust.

Both sides appear equally ravaged; ironically, dead men from
both sides are now next to each other as if cohorts, equally
faceless and equally degraded in the dirt.

Book five is "Diomedes Fights the Gods," and here
numerous gods become involved in the men's fighting. As this
section opens, Athena gives Diomedes "strength and daring"
but also, then, much more than this: "She set the man ablaze,
his shield and helmet flaming/with tireless fire ... /such fire
Athena blazed from Tydides' head and shoulders,/drove him
into the center where the masses struggled on." Still there are
two Trojans who readily surge forward to attack this
superhuman blaze. Nearly immediately Diomedes kills one,
and the other only escapes with the help of Ares, the war god.
For the Trojans who witness the assault on two of their great
men, "all their hearts were stunned."

Intent on aiding the Argives further, Athena convinces Ares not to interfere. Then Achaean captains each kill a key Trojan. The narrative describes this for about fifty lines and includes such vivid and gruesome details as:

> the famous spearman struck behind his skull,
> just at the neck-cord, the razor spear slicing
> straight up through the jaws, cutting away the tongue—
> he sank in the dust, teeth clenching the cold bronze.

Such descriptions occur throughout the epic. Frequent, also, are instances where men put themselves at great personal risk, either to strip a dead man of his armor so the killer can keep it as a trophy of his skill, or to save the body of a dead man who had been in one's own army, so it cannot be mutilated further but can be respectfully buried. Similarly not uncommon is the mention of fate as a key determiner. Each man has a fate, the characters believe, yet it is unclear for most what that is and when and how significant elements of it, such as a man's death, are to occur. In the case of Achilles, saving the body of a dead man and contemplating one's fate are more intense than they are for the average man.

The action returns to the rampaging Diomedes, who is hit by an arrow from Pandarus, the Trojans' best archer. Diomedes prays to Athena for help; she comes to his aid and tells him she's now given him the power to distinguish gods from men and that the only god he dare fight is Aphrodite. Revitalized, Diomedes charges, as "triple the fury seized him," and kills Trojans one after the other. Aeneas, a Trojan captain and son of Aphrodite, searches for Pandarus, attempting to inspire him to aim an arrow at Diomedes, yet the archer explains that Diomedes must have a god near him the way he is wildly charging and appears unharmed by the first arrow that was a direct hit.

But Aeneas will not be deterred and convinces Pandarus to join him in his chariot and destroy Diomedes. The two set off, but with Athena's help, Diomedes kills Pandarus, and Aeneas suffers a very serious blow from a massive boulder Diomedes hurls at him. With this, Aphrodite swoops in to save Aeneas, and Diomedes chases after her and wounds her. Apollo, "lord of the silver bow," now joins in to save Aeneas, but the narrative breaks from the tension of the battlefield and moves to Mount Olympus, as Aphrodite rushes to her mother for soothing.

After nearly one hundred lines of narrative about events on Mount Olympus, we are returned to Diomedes, just where we had left him earlier, charging Aeneas, who is still under the protection of Apollo. Despite Apollo, Diomedes repeatedly attacks and only "pulled back, just a little," after Apollo shrieks at him and emits a terrifying warning that he can never win against the gods. Apollo takes Aeneas from the fighting and replaces him with an Aeneas look-alike. Apollo calls, "Ares, Ares,/destroyer of men, reeking blood, stormer of ramparts,/can't you go and drag that man from the fighting?/That daredevil Diomedes, he'd fight Father Zeus!" Instead of directly following this plea, "murderous" Ares "whipped" the Trojans' "war-lust." Additionally, Apollo returns Aeneas, healed by the gods, back to the lines, inspiring the Trojans further. Still, the Achaeans are strong, and their captains remain powerful, killing numerous enemies.

Yet now joining in against the Achaeans are Ares and the "deadly Queen Enyo/ bringing Uproar on." Ares charges, staying close by Hector, and Diomedes is finally shaken, enough to tell the nearby men to give up ground while still facing the Trojans. Yet the fighting remains intense, and as Hector and Apollo kill more and more, Hera and Athena see they must intervene. Hera admonishes the Achaeans for being such poor warriors, reminding them that under Achilles this never would have happened (this being a clear reminder to the reader as well that the great Achilles remains waiting in the wings).

Athena rushes to Diomedes, climbing into his chariot, angered with Ares, who she says had only shortly before promised her and Hera that he would fight against the Trojans. Athena covers herself in darkness as the chariot storms for Ares. She saves Diomedes from a flying spear, and then when

Diomedes throws his own at Ares, she "rammed it home," causing Ares to "let loose a shriek, roaring,/thundering loud as nine, ten thousand combat soldiers." Book five ends at Olympus, where Ares has rushed for healing and where Hera and Athena return, the last lines telling us they "had stopped the murderous Ares' cutting men to pieces."

Book six, "Hector Returns to Troy," opens on the battlefield, continuing with the battle where the previous book had left off. One after another of the Argive captains strike down Trojan soldiers. Something unusual occurs as well, when for a brief moment Menelaus pities an enemy who is helpless before him and pleading for mercy.

The Trojans fall back. In an attempt to reverse this bad fortune, Helenus, another of King Priam's sons, advises Aeneas and Hector they must rally their troops. He says that Hector should go back to the city and tell his mother to make sacrifices to Athena on their army's behalf. Again we are reminded of Achilles, when Helenus remarks that Diomedes "is the strongest Argive now, I tell you./Never once did we fear Achilles so,/ ... But here's a maniac run amok—/no one can match his fury man-to-man!" The heroic Achilles' reputation has shrunk, then.

Hector rallies the troops so successfully that the Argives fall back, assuming a god must be aiding the Trojans now. In another part of the field, Diomedes questions whether he should move back as well, asking if a god is before him ready to attack or, if this is a man, that he explain who he is. Diomedes' confronter, who turns out to be one of the few men to exhibit modesty, explains that really all men equally are born and die. He then describes, in an unexpectedly lengthy seventy-five lines, his royal heritage. Diomedes exclaims, "Splendid—you are my friend,/my guest from the days of our grandfathers long ago!" He explains their connection to the noble man, Glaucus, and proposes that they avoid each other in battle. They "clasped each other's hands and traded pacts of friendship"— revealing a completely new aspect of Diomedes' personality, indicating that even a ravaging warrior respects heritage.

Indeed the contrast between humanity's warmth/love and its

horror is emphasized throughout this section. Next, for example, Hector instructs his mother to organize the older women and promise great offerings to Athena if the goddess will keep Diomedes from their city. Hector's mother's first words to him, contrasting his image as the great shining warrior are "[m]y child," as she remarks that he is worn out and offers him a drink.

Hector then lashes out at Paris, who agrees to join the fighting. Hector's last stop is to see his wife, Andromache, and their son. Hector breaks into a "broad smile" as he focuses on their "darling," "radiant" baby. Yet Andromache cries and chastises him for his recklessness, questioning if he has any pity for his son and "widow," since she says she knows Hector soon will be killed.

Hector says he must fight rather than die of shame, and he ominously states that he knows all in Troy must die. When he reaches for his son, the boy cringes in fear of the armor, although both parents laugh. Hector tries to comfort his wife, but as he leaves, those in his home perform dirges for the dead, convinced he will not return. Again, in contrast, Paris prepares for the battlefield, "exultant, laughing out loud," and as he joins up with Hector, the previously pessimistic man sounds hopeful.

Hector and Paris sweep down to the battlefield as **book seven**, "Ajax Duels with Hector," opens, and Athena and Apollo look on and devise a plan to have the men stop fighting for at least a day. Athena gets a message to Hector that he must propose a duel and that he should have no fear, since he will be safe for its duration. Hector moves out from the ranks and the fighting stops; he asks for a competitor to challenge him, but all Argives are afraid. Then Menelaus says he will take on Hector, yet Agamemnon stops him, saying even Achilles "dreads to pit himself against him." Menelaus gives in, and Nestor so successfully urges the other men to volunteer that nine do so.

Great Ajax is chosen by lot, "thrilled" to fight, while Hector now is in great fear. They engage in combat and Ajax leads, finally striking Hector down with a large boulder. Yet Apollo brings Hector back to his feet, and the two men would "have closed with swords, hacked each other," except that one man from each army comes forward and says they should stop and "yield to night." All are relieved.

Both camps strategize. At the Argives' meeting the captains agree to follow Nestor's suggestion to call a stop to the fighting so the men can gather and burn their dead comrades. Nestor advises that this would also give them time to build "looming ramparts" with gates and a trench in front, so their ships will have some protection.

On the Trojan side, the men are "shaken," and Antenor proposes that they return to the Argives Helen and all her treasures Paris had absconded. He reminds them: "We broke our sworn truce. We fight as outlaws." Paris refuses to consent but does offer to return the treasure as well as add more of his own.

The Trojan heralds go to the Achaean ships and announce the proposal, stating that Paris will not give up Helen, "though all Troy commands him to do precisely that." In response, "a hushed silence went through all the ranks," but Diomedes yells to the Argive men, "No one touch the treasures of Paris, Helen either!/It's obvious—any fool can see it. Now, at last/ the neck of Troy's in the noose—her doom is sealed." With that, "All the Achaean soldiers roared out their assent" and Agamemnon tells the Trojans that is their answer, adding "It is my pleasure too."

The next day, the men come together and collect the dead bodies, "weeping warm tears," with "their hearts breaking." The bodies are burned, the Achaeans create their wall and trench, "but all night long the Master Strategist Zeus/plotted fresh disaster for both opposing armies—/his thunder striking terror—/and blanching panic swept across the ranks."

Book eight, "The Tide of Battle Turns," begins at dawn. Zeus summons the gods and insists that none interfere with the human battle, so he "can bring this violent business to an end." He enumerates monstrous threats of what will happen to any who dare violate his orders and then returns to his throne. There he uses a golden scale to decide which army should take the lead, and when it tips in the Trojans' favor he hurls lightning towards the Achaeans, who "looked on in horror. White terror seized them all."

The Achaean leaders realize they cannot persist. Nestor becomes vulnerable on the battlefield, and when Diomedes comes to his aid, Diomedes urges the older man to ride in his chariot and that they attack Hector directly together. They charge. Yet Zeus creates great thunder and launches a spear of lightning directly at their horses' hooves. Nestor realizes they cannot fight the will of Zeus, but he has to work to convince Diomedes of this. At the same time Zeus sends more warnings. Diomedes doesn't want to turn back but wonders if they must, while Hector proclaims to his men that triumph is theirs.

Queen Hera is outraged, yet when she approaches Poseidon for support he says she must be mad to consider going against Zeus. Hector pushes the Achaeans back to their ships and is poised to set them on fire, when in desperation Agamemnon pleads to Zeus for help. Zeus pities the Argives and sends an eagle as a positive sign, inspiring them to charge forward with renewed vigor. Their great archer Teucer successfully strikes down many men but despite his continued efforts cannot harm Hector. When Teucer kills Hector's chariot driver, Hector goes directly for the archer, wounding him badly, yet Ajax and other Achaeans fight to protect Teucer and bring him to safety. Again Zeus "fired up the Trojans," and the Achaeans retreat in panic to their ships. Hector follows and holds his horses before the Argive trench.

Hera now convinces Athena that they must intercede, and while Athena says Zeus is proceeding this way only to exalt Achilles, Hera still cannot refrain from helping the Achaeans. The two prepare their war gear, yet Zeus sees and sends a messenger to warn them of the disastrous consequences if they interfere. With this, finally Hera advises Athena that they stop. Zeus admonishes them, and Hera says they will stay clear but only offer the Argives helpful tactics. Zeus says that the next day "still more hordes, whole armies of Argive soldiers" will be destroyed and that it will not stop until Achilles "rises," when the armies are "pinned in the fatal straits/and grappling for the body of Patroclus."

Night falls and so the fighting stops. Hector tells his men great victory will be theirs and decides they will camp close by the Achaean ships. They create blazing watch fires and instruct those behind the walls of Troy to do the same. They wait, among a thousand bright fires, spirits soaring.

In **book nine**, "The Embassy to Achilles," Agamemnon, with "streaming tears," tells the Achaean troops that since there is no chance of victory, they must return home. All are silent. Diomedes chastises the king for having no courage and for assuming all of them lack it as well. The armies shout their agreement, but then Nestor judiciously advises that the senior chiefs meet privately.

At the meeting Nestor proposes that they try to convince Achilles to fight again. Agamemnon agrees, calling what he did to Achilles "acts of madness." He enumerates a long list of gifts for Achilles: some of Agamemnon's own treasures; women; the woman Agamemnon took from Achilles, Briseis; a chance for Achilles to fill his ship with whatever he wants when they sack Troy; marriage to any of his daughters; and seven citadels to rule.

After an extensive description of the gifts, though, Agamemnon reveals that his feelings toward Achilles haven't changed:

> "All this—
> I would extend to him if he will end his anger.
> Let him submit to me! Only the god of death
> is so relentless, Death submits to no one—
> so mortals hate him most of all the gods.
> Let him bow down to me! I am the greater king,
> I am the elder-born, I claim—the greater man."

The scholar Cedric Whitman has written about Homer's characters and specifically Agamemnon: "Homer's sense of character is always profound, but Agamemnon is a consummate masterpiece.... [H]e is a magnificently dressed incompetence, without spirit or spiritual concern; his dignity is marred by pretension; his munificence by greed, and his prowess by a savagery which is the product of a deep uncertainty and fear. Yet none of this is ever overtly stated.... It is part of the tragedy that Agamemnon never meets with full disgrace, or understands himself really at all."

Nestor, while respected for his wisdom, in this case fails to realize what Achilles really would want to join the battle. He enlists Ajax, Phoenix, and Odysseus as messengers. Achilles warmly greets the three men, and Odysseus speaks first. He does not mention the gifts from Agamemnon immediately but explains what dire straits the Argives are in and what grief it will bring to Achilles the rest of his life if he lets the Trojans destroy them. He reminds Achilles of what his father must have told him before he set off for war—to keep in check his "proud, fiery spirit." Odysseus tells the warrior that the men will honor him, "like a god," when he saves them and that he will have his chance to kill Hector.

But Achilles will not budge, saying of Agamemnon: "I hate this man like the very Gates of Death/who says one thing but hides another in his heart." This is the crux of the matter, then; Achilles is looking for a change in Agamemnon's perspective toward him; not only does the king not respect him but he has belittled him in front of all the men. But aside from being intransigent, Achilles voices another attitude, one unexpectedly unheroic:

"No, what lasting thanks in the long run
for warring with our enemies, on and on, no end?
One and the same lot for the man who hangs back
and the man who battles hard. The same honor waits
for the coward and the brave. They both go down to Death,
the fighter who shirks, the one who works to exhaustion.

Similarly, later he insists, "I say no wealth is worth my life! ... / ... a man's life breath cannot come back again." Also very unheroically, he says he has no desire to battle Hector. The words cause us to question the definition of heroism and to be hopeful about humanity, since even the most vicious warrior can doubt the value of fighting.

Achilles' complains that Agamemnon avoids fighting but keeps most of the war booty and took back Briseis, the woman Achilles has grown to love. He says he and his men will sail home at dawn. He reveals something else here as well, which certainly would affect his perspective—his goddess mother has told him that he has two possible fates, one being if he fights he will die by Troy but remain in glory forever and the other being that if he goes back home he will have no glory but a long life.

After Achilles repeats that he will not help, Phoenix bursts into tears and pleads with him. Achilles still refuses the pleas, although now he concedes slightly and says they will decide in the morning if his troops will leave. Ajax, too, makes an ineffective appeal. But Achilles does make another concession, as now he says he will not fight until Hector arrives at their ships and sets them on fire.

Curiously, it is Diomedes who is most astute about Achilles' personality. When he hears Achilles' response, Diomedes says that offering so many gifts would never sway a proud man and that Achilles will fight, "in his own good time."

In **book ten**, "Marauding Through the Night," Agamemnon cannot sleep, in great fear of what morning will bring for his troops. He decides to go to Nestor for advice, and as he prepares to leave, his brother Menelaus arrives, also in anguish over their future. Agamemnon decides they must gather all the captains and also check that their guards are all still alert. In the meantime, he goes to rouse Nestor first, who says Zeus will never let Hector win and if Achilles decides to fight again, for sure Hector is in trouble. Nestor also voices his disappointment in Menelaus for making Agamemnon take on all the work. Agamemnon explains that he, too, is disappointed in Menelaus, who often "hangs back," "waiting for me/to make the first move." The complaints seem unjustified in light of what's occurred in the earlier duels and even more so in light of the fact that Menelaus was awake this night before Agamemnon. While we already see Agamemnon as self-centered and so are not too surprised at his comments, here, again, Nestor, in all his wisdom, is shown as misjudging, although his remarks about Hector and Achilles will prove directly on target.

At the captain's meeting, Nestor proposes that they send a man to spy on the Trojans and discover what they're planning. Diomedes volunteers and takes Odysseus with him, and Athena sends a positive sign so they know she's there to help them. In the meantime, Hector is meeting with his chiefs, and he, too, asks for a volunteer to spy on the enemy. He promises to give the man Achilles' chariot and horses, and the volunteer, Dolon, sets off but is quickly discovered by Odysseus. When caught, Dolon readily tells the two Achaeans all he knows, even suggesting the most vulnerable units they might take advantage of. While the man begs for his life, Diomedes beheads him with "a flashing hack."

At the Thracian camp, the one Dolon has described as most vulnerable and whose king has the best horses, Diomedes kills thirteen men in their sleep, including the king, while Odysseus moves their bodies so the horses may get through. When Odysseus is ready with the horses, Diomedes still is compelled to destroy more, but Athena warns that they must rush off. Apollo awakens a Thracian captain, and he and the other men break into sobs, now "swirled in panic," taking in "the grisly work the marauders did." In contrast, the two Argives return to their camp and are heartily welcomed by their captains; they wash, eat, and rest, "exultant."

Good fortune stays with the Argives the next morning, when Zeus instills their troops with great fury at the beginning of **book eleven**, "Agamemnon's Day of Glory." Many lines describe Agamemnon himself gearing up for battle. The Argives find renewed strength, and Agamemnon springs forth, killing many, "[l]ike devouring fire roaring down onto dry dead timber."

Zeus keeps Hector safe from Agamemnon and sends him a message telling him he must keep his men fighting. But, he is told, when Hector sees that Agamemnon is wounded that is when Zeus will give Hector power and when he will be able to gain ground all the way to the Argive ships. Hearing this, Hector encourages his troops, yet still Agamemnon wrecks havoc on the Trojans. When caught off guard, though, he is hit badly, keeps fighting, but finally must be brought off the field. Hector takes his cue and moves in.

Odysseus calls to Diomedes that they should fight together; he agrees but says that Zeus is on the Trojans' side now. Hector charges straight for them, and Diomedes predicts disaster but manages to spear Hector and knock him down, yet only momentarily. Shortly after, Paris hits Diomedes with an arrow, forcing him off the field. Left by himself, Odysseus considers fleeing but instead fights off numerous Trojans. He gets hit, but Athena keeps it from being a dangerous blow. The Trojans again charge at him when they see his wound, and Ajax comes to his aid until he can be taken for help. Paris hits Machaon, one of the Argive healers, and he, too, most valuable to the troops, must be brought off the field. Now Zeus forces Ajax to retreat, although he continues fighting, for some time aided by Eurypylus, who also ends up seriously wounded by Paris.

Achilles has been watching the action from afar and calls for Patroclus, who comes "striding up like the deathless god of war/but from that moment on his doom was sealed." Achilles directs Patroclus to go to Nestor and see who he has just brought in, wounded, in his chariot.

Nestor invites Patroclus to sit, but he responds that he cannot take the time to do so, since Achilles is "quick to anger." He adds that Nestor knows Achilles, "that great and terrible man./Why, he'd leap to accuse a friend without a fault." Nestor, too, is quick to criticize Achilles: "Now why is Achilles so cast down with grief/for this or that Achaean winged by a stray shaft?/He has no idea of the anguish risen through the army!/ ... [B]rave as he is, he has no care,/no pity for our Achaeans." Nestor wishes he himself were younger, powerful like he used to be, and launches into describing a battle in which he was a hero years earlier.

Nestor reminds Patroclus that Patroclus' own father told him to give Achilles "sound advice, guide him." He tells Patroclus that he might be able to persuade Achilles to fight but if not that Patroclus should fight and lead the Myrmidon army; he should dress in Achilles' armor to alarm the enemy.

Patroclus rushes off to speak to Achilles but on the way sees the wounded Eurypylus, pities him and the other fighting Argives, and asks him if they have any chance of not all being killed. Eurypylus says the situation is indeed hopeless and asks Patroclus to help him, since he is trained in healing. Patroclus helps the captain to his shelter, stops the blood flowing from his wound, and helps subdue the pain. Patroclus, with his ready empathy, immediately helps and provides healing and so starkly contrasts Achilles, who will help only belatedly and by killing.

We return to the battle at the trench and rampart in **book twelve**, "The Trojans Storm the Rampart." We are reminded that the Argives never made sacrifices to the gods when they built their fortress, so it will not last long. Hector, "that invincible headlong terror," pushes the Achaeans back. Polydamas suggests to Hector that rather than risk having the men take their horses and chariots through the trenches that the troops charge through by foot together. Hector agrees, and the men press forward, but two great Achaean fighters, Polypoetes and Leonteus, fight at the gates "like wild boars" as other Argives at the wall's ledge hurl boulders down on the Trojans.

Polydamas sees an eagle flying with a snake, which it drops because the snake keeps attacking it; Polydamas decides this is an omen that the Trojans will lose. He tells Hector they must stop, but Hector lashes out that Zeus told him to charge; he accuses Polydamas of being a coward and warns him that if he convinces others to turn back or holds back himself that "at one quick stroke my spear will beat you down,/you'll breathe your last!" Zeus helps the Trojans again by whipping a dust storm against the ships. Inspired by this, the Trojans work madly to tear at the battlements, but only with additional help from Zeus do they make headway. Zeus inspires his own son Sarpedon to charge the wall; Sarpedon calls to Glaucus for help.

The Achaean Menestheus cringes as he sees the Trojans coming, and he sends an aid to find Great Ajax and ask him for help. Ajax arrives, along with his brother the great archer Teucer, who hits Glaucus as he's climbing the wall. Glaucus jumps down quickly, trying to keep others from realizing he's taken a blow. Sarpedon does wrench down the wall, making "a gaping breach for hundreds." Teucer and Ajax immediately aim for Sarpedon and Teucer hits him, but Zeus saves him from death. Trojans swarm to Sarpedon's aid, fighting harder, but the Achaeans cannot be forced back. "Everywhere—rocks, ramparts, breastworks, swam/with the blood of Trojans, Argives, both sides," and neither gains on the other. Finally Zeus aids Hector again, and the leader smashes a boulder through the front gates. The Trojans now are streaming in at his command and "Argives scattering back in terror,/back by the hollow hulls, the uproar rising, no way out, no end—."

Zeus leaves the men "to bear the brunt/and wrenching work of war—no end in sight—," in **book thirteen**, "Battling for the Ships." He never suspects that a god would go against his earlier orders, but his brother Poseidon pities the Argives and interferes with the battle, giving renewed power to Great and Little Ajax and inspiring the Achaean troops. The troops press together, forming a wall against the Trojans, so that even Hector is pushed back by their stabbing line of swords. Hector and Ajax meet, but Ajax cannot wound Hector, although he does press him back from the ships.

Poseidon continues urging the Achaeans and disguises himself as a mortal so he also can spur on Idomeneus, captain of the Cretans, who has temporarily left the battlefield. Idomeneus meets his friend Meriones, who is in need of a new spear; both talk of their courage, and Idomenus gives a comparison of his definitions of a coward and a brave man. Curiously, the brave man, in his view, is not just brave but "prays to wade in carnage, cut-and-thrust at once." When the Trojans see Idomeneus and Meriones arriving back at the battle, they surge forward. Fierce fighting ensues—"storming chaos, troops inflamed,/slashing each other with bronze, carnage mounting,/ ... Only a veteran steeled at heart could watch that struggle/and still thrill with joy and never feel the terror."

Poseidon continues to spur the Argives and Idomeneus, and the Trojans panic. The Trojan Deiphobus, enraged over a friend's death, strikes back but misses Idomeneus, who strikes down other Trojans and then taunts Deiphobus to take him on directly. But the Trojan thinks better of it and calls Aeneas to help, prompting Idomeneus to call for help as well, and then Aeneas to call for more help. Idomeneus and Aeneas fight, aiming "to hack each other's flesh." Neither is successful at wounding the other, but numerous men die in brutal deaths and the war continues relentlessly.

Menelaus rushes in when he sees a comrade killed, and Pisander rushes at him; then Menelaus "hacked Pisander between the eyes,/the bridge of the nose, and bone cracked, blood sprayed/and both eyes dropped at his feet to mix in the dust—." With this, Menelaus yells at the Trojans for stealing his wife and riches. He calls out to Zeus, and accuses him—"all this brutal carnage comes from *you*." He rails at Zeus for favoring the Trojans, charging "no one can glut their lust for battle!"

The fighting continues, "like a mass of whirling fire." Through it all, Hector keeps driving on, unaware that his men are struggling now that the Achaeans have been revived. In fact, the Argives are even near victory on the left of the battle area. Polydamas rushes to Hector, warning that they are in great trouble, advising that they draw back and meet with the captains to create a plan. Hector rushes off to do so and learns from his brother Paris that the captains are dead, except for two that have been wounded and taken from the field. Zeus has masses of men follow Hector in a new surge. Ajax taunts Hector, and he responds with his own barbs, then rushes on the Achaeans, who remain undaunted.

In **book fourteen**, "Hera Outflanks Zeus," Old Nestor goes to a look-out point to see how the war is progressing and is stunned to see the desecration. The wounded kings also are coming to look, and Nestor tells them the great wall is destroyed and the enemy is storming. Agamemnon suggests that they wait until night and leave in their ships. Yet Odysseus condemns the idea, calling not the war but Agamemnon the disaster. Diomedes says they should go back into battle, even though they are wounded, and at least encourage the men. The others agree.

Poseidon returns, now to inspire these men. He sends a message to Agamemnon telling him that, unlike Achilles, Agamemnon has not enraged the gods and he will see the Trojans retreat in fear for their lives. Hera is joyful at seeing Poseidon helping the Achaeans and wishes she could join in as well. She tricks Aphrodite into giving her the power to induce love and longing. Next she approaches Sleep, asking him to put Zeus to sleep after she makes love with him. Even after she's offered Sleep gifts, he turns her down, in fear of what Zeus would do to him if he agreed to her plan. Yet when Hera offers Sleep his pick of any of the younger Graces to take as his wife, he cannot resist and agrees to help her.

Hera finds Zeus, and he immediately lusts for her. As planned, after they make love he is put to sleep. Sleep also informs Poseidon of what's happened, so he can help the Argives even more. Poseidon inspires and advises the men, and the armies clash. Once again Ajax and Hector confront each other, but this time Ajax's blow to Hector sends him "whirling off like a whipping-top,/reeling round and round." Hector falls, and Achaeans rush in to attack further, but the Trojans fend them off, having already surrounded their great hero. Hector is whisked away in a chariot, and when its drivers stop and splash water on him from the nearby river, "he crouched down on his knees to vomit dark clots/then slumped back down, stretched on the ground again/and the world went black as night across his eyes."

Meanwhile the Argives charge harder, and Polydamas and Ajax yell back and forth with threats and warnings. Ajax and other Achaeans slaughter many, and the Trojans flee.

Yet the Trojans are not in trouble for long. In **book fifteen**, "The Achaean Armies at Bay," Zeus wakes up and sees Hector seriously wounded, vomiting blood. Zeus screams at Hera for being so treacherous, yet she denies she's had anything to do with the Trojan sufferings, saying the god of the earthquakes has been working against the Trojans but not with her help. Zeus believes her, tells her to get Apollo and Iris, the messenger, and also tells Hera his plan: Hector will push the Achaeans back to their ships; Achilles will send Patroclus into the battle, where he will kill many, including Zeus' son Sarpedon; Hector will kill Patroclus; Achilles will finally fight, killing Hector; and the Achaeans will become unstoppable until they seize Troy.

Hera sends Apollo and Iris to Zeus, where they get their orders. Iris gives Poseidon Zeus' message that he must no longer intervene for the Achaeans, and while he is livid at hearing this, he takes Iris' advice and says he will stop, even though he says he and Zeus are equals, being brothers.

Apollo follows Zeus' orders to panic the Argives and instill great courage in Hector. First Apollo heals Hector, who's still struggling on the sidelines. The god tells Hector he will clear the way for the Trojans' assault on the Argives. Hector responds with great vigor, and the Argives give ground. Thoas, a great Achaean spearman, tells the others it's a miracle that Hector is back, that a god must have helped him, and that they must band together with their greatest champions in front, which they do, bravely packed and standing their ground. Yet when Apollo looks the Achaeans in the eyes and "loosed an enormous battle cry himself," the Argives panic, and are routed. Many are killed, and Hector commands his men to storm the ships.

Patroclus, still trying to soothe the wounded Eurypylus, hears the Trojans storm the wall and says he must go and try to convince Achilles to fight. The Argives block the Trojans but cannot push them back from the ships. Hector and Ajax, too, fight and keep each other from gaining. A Trojan comes forward with a torch of fire, yet Ajax stabs him dead. Hector's spear hits a friend of Ajax's near him, and Ajax calls to his brother Teucer for help. Teucer responds, and even when he realizes that a god has interfered by destroying his bow, he remains undaunted, taking up a spear at Ajax's suggestion. Hector sees the destroyed bow and calls out to his men that Zeus is fighting for them, but each time he inspires his troops Ajax does the same on his side. Zeus is watching, waiting for the first ship to be set on fire, and again we are told that that is when Zeus will work in the Argives' favor, finally giving them great glory. The fact that we have been told this more than once never ruins the suspense of the epic, a tribute to its mastery. We are told, too, that Hector will soon die.

The Achaeans withstand the onslaught and "never flinched in fear," until Hector charges at their main force "all afire,/blazing head to foot." The Trojans storm by the ships, and the Achaeans are forced back from the front ships but hold their ground at the nearby tents, encouraged by Nestor. Zeus presses the Trojans on in another "desperate battle" at the ships, and the Argives fear they will lose their lives, as the Trojans' "hopes soared," "closing for the kill." Hector calls for fire, but Ajax, "tensing, braced," spears each man that comes forward with it, all the while yelling encouragement to his cohorts.

Patroclus, in tears, returns to Achilles in **book sixteen**, "Patroclus Fights and Dies." He informs Achilles of all the losses the Achaeans have suffered and that their greatest men have been wounded. He scorns Achilles: "But *you* are intractable, Achilles!/Pray god such anger never seizes *me*, such rage you nurse./Cursed in your own courage!" He adds that if Achilles has been told his fate is doomed and this has kept him from the battle then he should at least let Patroclus go in his place and lead his Myrmidon army. Achilles responds that no prophecy holds him back, just the humiliation Agamemnon inflicted upon him. He selfishly tells Patroclus he should fight, so Patroclus can "win great honor, great glory" for Achilles. He warns him to leave the battle once the Trojans are fought back from the Achaean ships and not chase the Trojans back to their city, since one of the gods may step in to help the Trojans.

The narrative returns to Ajax, still holding Trojans off from the ship decks but now exhausted since Zeus has stepped in to help the enemies. "Again and again/," we are told, Ajax "fought for breath, gasping, bathed in sweat/rivering down his body.... " Hector moves in, destroys Ajax's weapon, and Ajax knows the gods are against him and moves back. The Trojans now light the ships.

Now the narrative reverts to Achilles, and we find that Patroclus prepares for battle, donning Achilles' gear, as Achilles rounds up the Myrmidon troops. As the troops head into the battle, Achilles prays to Zeus, and we learn again that Patroclus will drive the Trojans back but not return alive. In the meantime, Patroclus has roused the men, and when the Trojans see them coming, they believe Patroclus is Achilles and panic. Patroclus kills a chief of one of the Trojans' allies, "whipping terror in all their hearts." He pushes men off the ships and stops the fire, but the Trojans, although losing ground, still fight and hold the Achaeans in a deadlock. The Argive captains are revived, and such strides are made against the enemy that the Trojans turn to flee, Hector included. Patroclus continues rampaging, striking men down at every turn.

Sarpedon inspires his men to stop running and heads straight for Patroclus himself. Zeus, watching from afar, tells Hera how disturbed he is to know Sarpedon, his own son, is to be killed by Patroclus. He contemplates intervening, but Hera sways him against it. Patroclus strikes Sarpedon a great blow, leaving the man "sprawled and roaring, clawing the bloody dust" and calling to his friend Glaucus to save his body. Glaucus is still suffering from his wounds from Teucer's arrow, yet Apollo heals him and Glaucus spurs on Sarpedon's Lycian captains and their men, as well as Hector and other key leaders. The Trojans and their allies are in grief over Sarpedon's death and close in to save his corpse, but the Achaeans rally around Patroclus as well, all struggling for the body, until it is "covered over head to toe,/buried under a mass of weapons, blood and dust."

Zeus continues to survey the brutal scene and contemplate what should occur next. He decides to let Patroclus press the Trojans back to Troy and so has Hector turn cowardly and order his men to retreat. In the meantime, Apollo swoops down at Zeus' orders and rescues Sarpedon's body, so he may receive his rightful royal burial.

Patroclus does not heed Achilles' warning that he leave the battle once the Trojans have fled. In fact, Patroclus leads the Achaeans to Troy's gates, where they are almost victorious, but Apollo hurls Patroclus back repeatedly and then shrieks down at him to stop, since it is not his fate to topple Troy, nor is it

Achilles'. This is the first we've heard of limits being imposed on Achilles' fighting powers.

Patroclus finally moves back, and Apollo inspires Hector to attack the man. When Patroclus sees him coming, he aims his spear, which strikes Hector's driver, Cebriones. Patroclus taunts Cebriones' dead body; he springs forward to claim the corpse, but Hector jumps from his chariot toward the body as well, and many others join in the "grueling, maiming" fight.

The Achaeans manage to pull Cebriones' armor from his body, and Patroclus continues killing Trojans "like something superhuman," until Apollo slams him in the back and shoulders and strips him of his gear. A Dardan fighter spears Patroclus, and Hector spears him as well and glories over him, claiming "the vultures will eat your body raw!" Patroclus struggles for breath but still must respond, reminding Hector that he himself did not kill Patroclus and that even if twenty Hectors had charged him he'd have killed them all. He warns that Hector's death is soon to come. Patroclus dies, but Hector still must yell back. He pulls his spear from the dead man and then tries to kill Achilles' aide, but the aide escapes on Achilles' "magnificent racing stallions."

Menelaus sees Patroclus' sorry fate and plows through to protect the body from the enemy, in **book seventeen**, entitled "Menelaus' Finest Hour." Menelaus holds off the Trojans, but when Apollo urges Hector into the melee, Menelaus wonders if he should leave or, if he stays, how he will survive Hector's attack. Menelaus retreats from the body and finds Ajax, and the two return to retrieve the body but see Hector already stripping it of Achilles' great armor. When Hector sees the two Argives heading toward him, he falls back into his amassed men.

Glaucus rebukes Hector, saying Hector cares not for any of his allies if he is willing to let the dead body of Sarpedon, one of the greatest allies, be stolen by the Achaeans. Glaucus says if the Trojans can get Patroclus' body, then the Argives would give up Sarpedon's. He calls Hector a coward for shrinking from combat with Ajax. Angered, Hector dresses in Achilles' armor and rouses all his commanders, saying he will give "one half the bloody spoils" to the man who can retrieve Patroclus.

Zeus decides to give Hector great power, since his death is soon to come. Ajax sees Hector storming towards them and alerts Menelaus, who calls the Achaean captains. Zeus drives the Achaeans, and when the Trojans begin to pull Patroclus' corpse away, the great Ajax fights them off and most scatter. Hector attacks Ajax, and Ajax strikes back with such force that Trojans, including Hector, fall back. Again the Trojans would have clambered all the way to the safety of their city walls, defeated, if Apollo had not intervened. He speaks to Aeneas, who recognizes him at once and calls out to Hector, the Trojans, and their allies that Zeus impels them to fight. Now the armies engage in a great deadlock, as all day long "the fighting raged,/grim and grueling, relentless, drenching labor, nonstop."

Hector aims to take Achilles' immortal horses, calling Aeneas for help, and the Achaean captains gather to fend them off. Both of the Ajax men get the Trojans to back away, but then the fight returns to Patroclus' body. Zeus sends Pallas to urge on the Achaeans, but Apollo goes to Hector's side and then Zeus gives his favor to the Trojans. Ajax realizes Zeus is against them now, and in desperation Menelaus searches for a man to inform Achilles of what's happened to Patroclus. Menelaus finds Antilochus and sends him off, doubtful Achilles will come to their aid, especially, also, since he has no armor. Telemonian Ajax says Menelaus and Meriones should pick up Patroclus and that he and the other Ajax will protect them. The Trojans charge forward, but the two Ajax unnerve them. As the Achaeans struggle to get Patroclus to safety, "fighting flared behind them/wild as a flash fire, sprung out of nowhere." Argives flee.

In **book eighteen**, "The Shield of Achilles," Antilochus informs Achilles of Patroclus' terrible death. Achilles is grief-stricken, claws the ground, tears his hair, and weeps. The loud cries reach Achilles' mother, who rushes to him and asks what's wrong, relating that Zeus has done as he's promised: the Achaeans suffer great losses and are pinned against their ships because they do not have Achilles' help.

But Achilles explains that these events cannot bring him joy, since his most loved comrade is dead. He explains that "unending sorrows must surge" within her heart as well, since his own death is imminent, according to the prophecy, because he plans to soon kill Hector. He examines his actions and admonishes himself:

> nor did I bring one ray of hope to my Patroclus,
> nor to the rest of all my steadfast comrades,
> countless ranks struck down by mighty Hector—
> No, no, here I sit by the ships ...
> a useless dead weight on the good green earth—

Thetis tells Achilles that he cannot rush out to fight, since Hector has his armor; she promises to return the next day with new gear for him.

The narrative returns to the battlefield, where Achaeans are rushing back to their ships to escape Hector. Still men battle over Patroclus' corpse. Then Hera sends Iris to tell Achilles to enter the fight. When Achilles answers that he must wait for his new armor, Iris says he should go out to the trench to scare the Trojans. Pallas now helps by equipping Achilles with the "tremendous storm-shield," and "crowning his head the goddess swept a golden cloud/and from it she lit a fire to blaze across the field." Achilles stands at the trench and blasts "an enormous cry" and Pallas shrieks too, causing the Trojans to panic and run. Finally the Achaeans claim Patroclus' body.

The Trojan leaders meet to discuss what they can possibly do; they are terrified of Achilles. Polydamas says they must retreat to their gated city, but Hector is disgusted at the suggestion and says they must persist in the battle.

Thetis arrives at the home of Hephaestus, god of fire, and asks him for new gear for Achilles. The god is happy to help Thetis, since she saved his life when his own mother wanted to hide him because he was a cripple. Hephaestus creates a shield that is "a world of gorgeous immortal work." On it he shows the earth, sky, sea, sun, moon, constellations, and two cities. In one city is a great wedding party. But in the same streets where the party travels, an argument has broken out.

Around the second city there is an army split in two over whether to plunder the city or split its riches with its inhabitants. There is also a land being plowed, a king's estate where harvesters are bringing in grain, a thriving vineyard, a herd of cattle attacked by a pair of lions, a meadow. There is a dancing circle of young boys and girls beautifully dressed and a joyful crowd surrounding them. The scholar Bernard Knox observes, "These vivid pictures of normal life, drawn with consummate skill and inserted in a relentless series of gruesome killings, have a special poignancy; they are one of the features of Homer's evocation of battle which make it unique: an exquisite balance between the celebration of war's tragic, heroic values and those creative values of civilized life that war destroys."

We leave the artful beauty of the god's work and return to Achilles at the beginning of **book nineteen**, "The Champion Arms for Battle." His mother brings him his new dazzling armor and tells him to gather the Argive men, "renounce your rage at the proud commander Agamemnon," and quickly prepare for battle. She gives him "tremendous courage" and puts ambrosia in Patroclus, to keep his body from deteriorating, since Achilles has declared it will not be buried until Hector's body is beside it.

When all the men are gathered, Achilles addresses Agamemnon, asking whether it was worth it for them to have raged at each other, and then answers that it was worth it—for the Trojans. He proclaims that he will drive off his anger and lead the men into battle. All cheer. Agamemnon says that the armies would often revile him for his fight with Achilles, but that he cannot be blamed, since the gods drove him into "savage madness." He says all the gifts he had offered Achilles earlier are now his.

Achilles urges that they quickly prepare for the battlefield, but Odysseus firmly counsels that the troops must eat, that the gifts can be brought out for all to see, that Agamemnon swear he never touched Briseis. He advises also that Achilles "show some human kindness too, in your own heart" and that Agamemnon "be more just to others." Achilles still urges that they fight without food, but Odysseus sways him against this. The gifts are brought out, Agamemnon swears he never touched Briseis, and Achilles blames Zeus for Agamemnon's fight with him as well.

Briseis returns and cries out in pain at the sight of Patroclus' body, calling her life "one endless sorrow!" Finally, rather than just being a pawn, she has a chance to speak, and whereas Achilles has repeatedly proclaimed his love for her, here she speaks of her great affection for Patroclus, who helped her when Achilles killed her husband and plundered her homeland, on the same day when her three brothers were killed as well. We don't even see Achilles' reaction to having Briseis back, and while many gather around him trying to assuage his grief, it seems Briseis actually has suffered more losses. Not too many lines later we are also reminded of others' suffering: "His [Achilles'] voice rang out in tears and the warlords mourned in answer,/each remembering those he had left behind at home." These lines, of course, also are a reminder of another life far away from deadly battle—home life, a place of comfort and where young lives are nourished.

At Zeus' request, Athena gives Achilles ambrosia and nectar, since he's refused to eat. He dresses in his new glorious gear, and "his eyes blazed forth in searing points of fire." His horses are readied, and Hera has one speach, telling him they will save his life this time but that he still is doomed to die, "cut down by a deathless god and mortal man!"

The Argives fall into battle formation, while on Olympus Zeus calls all gods to meet. This is **book twenty**, "Olympian Gods in Arms," where Zeus tells the other gods that they should go and help whichever army they wish. He believes if Achilles is left unchecked he'll raze the walls of Troy, defying fate. The gods speed down, as Achilles is winning glory for the Argives. Athena erupts in her "stunning war cry," and Ares does the same, each on an opposite warring side. Zeus lets loose great thunder; Poseidon shakes the earth, and each of the other gods join in, creating an immense clash.

At the same time, Achilles is intent on destroying Hector. However, Aeneas faces Achilles first, pressed on by the gods Phoebus and Apollo, while the other gods stay on the sidelines temporarily. Achilles taunts Aeneas, quite at length, trying to logically discourage the man from a contest, saying Aeneas has nothing to gain since Priam will not give his throne to him even if he could prove himself a hero. Achilles also reminds Aeneas of their earlier battle, when Aeneas was only saved because the gods interfered. Aeneas yells back, pointing out that his mother is the goddess Aphrodite and explaining the rest of his lineage.

The fighting begins. Aeneas' weapon cannot penetrate Achilles' great shield, but Achilles' spear comes very close to hitting Aeneas. The god of earthquakes pulls Aeneas from the battle and orders him to stay away from the monstrous Achilles and only after Achilles' death move back into the front lines, since no other Argive can kill him.

Achilles returns to the lines and pushes each man to fight harder, as Hector does the same on his side. Apollo warns Hector not to challenge Achilles, and Hector moves back, "terrified," until he sees his own brother Polydorus killed by Achilles. Now Hector moves in, unflinching. Yet Athena turns his spear away from Achilles, and Phoebus, in turn, keeps Hector safe from Achilles' charging and spears, until the Argive realizes he must give up. Instead of pursuing Hector, Achilles rushes at numerous other Trojan men, killing continuously while "the earth ran black with blood."

The chase continues into **book twenty-one**, "Achilles Fights the River." The fleeing Trojans and storming Achilles reach a ford in the Xanthus River, and Achilles drives half of the Trojans back to the city, while the other half are forced into the water, flailing, screaming, spinning in its whirlpools. Achilles leaps into the water with his sword and slaughters Trojans, then stops and captures twelve men to be killed later, as he had promised he would do in partial recompense for Patroclus' death. He sends them off with his comrades and then whirls back to the water, "insane to hack more flesh."

The first man he confronts, Lycaon, is one he had caught

earlier; he's shocked that the man's still alive; the man is shocked that he's only been home for twelve days and fate has cast him in Achilles' path again. He says Zeus must hate him and begs Achilles to spare his life, but Achilles says that while he had taken many prisoners before, now that Patroclus is dead he will kill as many Trojans as possible. He tells Lycaon that he must die and that even one as glorious as Achilles himself is fated to die in this battle.

Achilles plunges his sword into Lycaon and charges after more men, crying: "Die, Trojans, die—/till I butcher all the way to sacred Troy—/run headlong on, I'll hack you from behind!" The river is angry now and inspires Asteropaeus to confront the Argive hero. Achilles asks for the man's background, and we learn that he is the leader of the Paeonian troops and that he comes "from the Axius' broad currents." He hurls two spears together at Achilles, and one draws blood from the hero's arm. But Achilles slices the man to death and over his corpse explains that he had to win, since his father is the son of Aeacus, who sprang from Zeus, who is stronger than any stream.

Achilles continues the slaughter until the river tells him to stop and at least not kill men in his water. While Achilles agrees, the river is not content with this and calls Apollo to help the Trojans. But when Achilles hears this, he plunges back in and the water rages against him, until Achilles desperately calls to Zeus for help. Poseidon and Athena swoop in and drive Achilles on, yet the Xanthus refuses to back down and calls Simois for help. Hera calls her son Hephaestus to help Achilles, and the god shoots fires into the plain, along the banks of the river, and into the river itself, which "screamed in flames."

Xanthus cries to Hera to stop the fire, and she does, but now the other gods join in, colliding in a "mammoth clash," with Zeus only laughing, "delighted." Athena knocks down Ares and Aphrodite. Poseidon challenges Apollo to fight, but Apollo flees, and when his sister Artemis chastises him, Hera attacks her. The gods return to Olympus, except for Apollo, who is now in Troy, driving Prince Agenor to challenge the rampaging

Achilles. When Achilles springs at Agenor, Apollo whisks him to safety and disguises himself as the prince, drawing Achilles further and further from the city so the Trojans can make it back inside to safety.

The Trojans are inside their city, with Achaeans moving closer and Hector standing in front. This is the opening of **book twenty-two**, "The Death of Hector." Apollo, still with Achilles chasing him, finally reveals who he is, and the angered Achilles turns away and dashes toward the city. King Priam sees Achilles approaching and begs Hector to come inside the city walls. He reminds his son of how many sons of his Achilles has already killed. His wife joins him in pleading with Hector and weeping.

Hector considers returning to the gates but fears his men will lash out at him for ruining their army and not returning to safety earlier, all because of his "own reckless pride." He evaluates another option as well, which is to take off his armor, meet Achilles, and offer to return Helen and all her riches and to share Troy's riches as well. Hector realizes, though, that Achilles would "show no mercy,/no respect for me, my rights—he'll cut me down/straight off."

Achilles approaches, and Hector trembles and runs. Achilles chases him around the walls of Troy, as Zeus watches with the other gods and wonders if Hector, whom he loves, should be saved. Hector hopes someone from Troy may help him, but Achilles orders that no Achaeans help Achilles because "someone might snatch the glory, Achilles come in second." Apollo gives Hector strength to keep running, but Zeus consults his sacred golden scales and they show Hector as the loser. Apollo leaves Hector, and Athena rushes to Achilles.

The goddess tells Achilles that Zeus is on their side. She goes to Hector, disguises herself as Deiphobus, Hector's brother, and proclaims that together they can kill the Achaean warrior. Hector is moved that someone is brave enough to help him, making Athena's trick appear even more cruel, especially when she embellishes by telling Hector how the others begged Deiphobus not to go but he insisted. When Achilles is finally near, Hector explains that if he wins he will take Achilles' armor but will not mutilate his body. He says he will return it to the Achaeans. He tells Achilles to swear he will do the same, but Achilles vehemently refuses.

Achilles throws the first spear and misses, but, unbeknownst to Hector, Athena retrieves it for him. Hector throws his spear, misses, and asks Deiphobus for another. When he sees that his brother is not there, he realizes he has been tricked and has no chance for survival. Still, he bravely charges with his sword. Achilles aims for a weak spot and hits Hector in the neck. He crashes to the ground, and Achilles "gloried over him." Hector begs him again to give his body to the Trojans, to which Achilles ruthlessly responds:

> Beg no more, you fawning dog—begging me by my parents!
> Would to god my rage, my fury would drive me now
> to hack your flesh away and eat you raw— ...
> The dogs and birds will rend you—blood and bone!

Hector gasps a few more words and then dies. Achilles still taunts Hector's body. The Achaeans move in, each stabbing Hector, and then Achilles ties him to the back of his chariot and drags him in the dirt at great speed. King Priam sees this and tries to rush after Achilles. Hecuba cries out for Hector. Hector's wife, who, poignantly, has ordered servants to draw a bath for him, finally, too, sees her husband's fate.

Back at the Achaean war ships, in **book twenty-three**, "Funeral Games for Patroclus," Achilles has his Myrmidons drive their chariots by Patroclus as the soldiers mourn. He treats the thousands of Myrmidons to a great feast but must leave himself when Agamemnon calls him to feast with him.

After the great meal, Achilles mourns and finally falls asleep. He is visited by Patroclus' ghost, who says Achilles must bury him quickly, since he wanders aimlessly, unable to join the other dead. Ultimately, then, not burying Patroclus immediately has only hurt the man. Patroclus cries that they will never be reunited and also requests that their bones be buried together. This, indeed, reinforces how strong their bond had been. He reminds Achilles how they grew up together, since Achilles' kind father took Patroclus in and appointed him Achilles' aide. Prior to this, Patroclus had been banished and left homeless, and now he remarks that he had been a fool for murdering a man because of a quarrel over a mere game of dice. This reminds us of Achilles' own quarrel with Agamemnon, which resulted not just in the death of his great friend but in the deaths of legions of soldiers as well.

In the morning, thousands of men process in Patroclus' funeral, but only the captains stay when the pyre is loaded with sheep, cattle, and other sacrifices, as well as the twelve Trojans Achilles had captured, that he now "hacked to pieces." He calls farewell to Patroclus, and his last words to him are that Hector will never get such a mourning since dogs will eat his flesh. But the stubborn Achilles does not know that the gods are working against him in this regard, protecting Hector's body from damage. Achilles prays to the gods for help in creating a good fire, and all night long they "hurled the flames ... blast on screaming blast," as Achilles drags himself around the pyre, "choked with sobs."

The next morning, men gather Patroclus' bones, and Achilles tells them they must be buried with his. Then, with all the armies gathered, Achilles announces that he will hold funeral games in honor of Patroclus. Men haul numerous prizes from his ships, and he explains that the first contest will be a chariot race. Men volunteer to race: Eumelus, Diomedes, Menelaus, and Antilochus. Antilochus is Nestor's son, and the old man offers him sage counsel on how to win the race. Meriones also joins the race.

The gods of war are quick to sway this contest as well, with Apollo working against Diomedes and Athena helping him as well as harming Eumelus. Antilochus is near to passing Menelaus, who calls him a maniac for moving in on him just as the track's ready to narrow, seriously jeopardizing their safety. Antilochus won't listen, so Menelaus drops behind to prevent a likely collision. The onlooking men can't see what's been happening since the chariots are too far away, but some men strain to see and report to the armies, although there are differences in opinion as to what's happening. Such an argument ensues that Achilles must intervene, curiously, as the peacemaker. Diomedes wins the race, with Antilochus coming in second, Menelaus very close behind, Meriones fourth, and Eumelus last. Achilles pities Eumelus and offers him second prize, causing Antilochus to balk in anger and say he won't give up his prize. Achilles smiles and gives in to Antilochus, and again we are reminded of Achilles' own anger when his prize was taken away from him when the epic started.

Menelaus charges Antilochus with deliberately blocking his chariot, and Antilochus quickly asks him for forgiveness, offering him his prize and any other he would like, so he may stay in his favor. Menelaus softens and says Antilochus is just still young. He says since Antilochus, his brother, and father have suffered and fought for him, he will give back the prize to show "the heart inside me is never rigid, unrelenting." Again, we are reminded of what has brought these men to the Trojan shores (to chase after Menelaus' wife) and of what has caused them so many losses (Achilles' own rigid, unrelenting heart, which contrasts with Menelaus'). Here, finally, we see value in good will, understanding, forgiveness, yielding. Achilles also offers a prize to Nestor, who is most grateful and describes incidents from his past when he was strong and young rather than in "the pains of old age." Achilles savors the stories, perhaps realizing his own strength and youth will soon only be remembered in stories.

Next is a boxing match between Epeus, the famous boxing champion, and Euryalus. Euryalus is caught off guard and knocked out, although Epeus graciously helps him up. Following is "the grueling wrestling-match" between Giant Ajax and Odysseus, who hold each other in a stalemate for some time. Then each throws the other with such force that Achilles stops the fight and tells them to share the prizes.

A footrace follows, during which Odysseus prays to Athena for help. She promptly assists him by having Oilean Ajax slip near the finish line on a pile of cow dung. The men laugh uproariously at Ajax, as his mouth and nostrils drip with the manure. Yet the comic relief is fleeting, for now the most frightening contest takes place between Telamonian Ajax and

Diomedes, who are to fight in full battle gear until blood is drawn and entrails reached. Again, the contest must be stopped, this time because the onlooking men scream for it when Diomedes gains great advantage. Next Achilles shows a lump of pig iron that the men must throw. Polypoetes is the last to hurl it and flings it so far beyond the others' that the armies roar.

In archery Teucer the master archer is challenged by Meriones, who wins because he swears to Apollo that he will sacrifice numerous animals for him. The final contest is spear-throwing, but when Agamemnon comes forward to compete, Achilles says they all know he is the best and tells him to take first prize, "if that would please your heart." Agamemnon "could not resist," but then graciously gives the prize to his herald Talthybius. There appears finally to be a truce between the king and Achilles.

The men return to their ships to eat and sleep in **book twenty-four**, "Achilles and Priam." Achilles, though, still grieves, and night after night cannot sleep but tries to comfort himself by dragging Hector behind his chariot, making circles around Patroclus' pyre site. Zeus decides Priam must give Achilles a ransom for Hector's body. This plan is explained to Achilles and Priam, and Priam is told he must travel with only one herald to the Achaean camp but that the god Hermes will protect him on his journey and Achilles will not kill him. The men set out and are terrified when they come upon Hermes, disguised as a traveler, who then reassures them that he will protect them. He explains that he is an aide of Achilles, asks Priam to pity his own sorry lot, and warns that the Achaeans are restless for more war. When they reach the Argive camp safely, Hermes finally reveals who he is, says he must leave, and advises the king to clasp Achilles' knees and implore him by his parents.

Priam follows the advice. Achilles says nothing but is deeply stirred, and then both men weep, Priam for Hector, and Achilles for his father and Patroclus. Achilles' first words show he pities Priam: "Poor man, how much you've borne—pain to break the spirit!" We know Achilles must be deeply moved, since he says they both must stop grieving, even though earlier it had seemed nothing could stop Achilles' grieving.

Priam says he must see his son with his own eyes and tells Achilles to take the ransom and return safely home with his ships. Achilles warns him not to anger him, since if he becomes too angry he may go against Zeus' plan. Priam is terrified, and Achilles leaves. He and his men take the ransom but leave some to shroud Hector's body. Achilles orders women to clean the body, so Priam will not become angry and in turn inspire Achilles' anger, which Achilles knows could cause him to kill the king. When the body is ready, Achilles himself lifts it onto a bier, and his friends help him place it in the wagon.

Achilles returns to Priam and tells him Hector's body is ready for him. While earlier Achilles' mother was concerned over his not eating and sleeping but mourning too much, now Achilles tells Priam they must eat. At the meal, each man looks at the other and marvels at his traits, and then Priam asks Achilles to let him sleep, since although he has not slept since his son has died he now knows he can. Similarly he remarks how he had not been able to eat but now could, reminding us of Achilles' own situation as well. Achilles asks the king how much time he will need to bury Hector, saying he will hold off warring until after then. Priam sleeps, and finally Achilles does as well, and we are told that Briseis is by his side, an additional sign of a return to normalcy.

Hermes awakens Priam and quickly ushers the men out to avoid danger. Morning comes as the two weeping men approach Troy. Once they are sighted, screams echo through the city. All stream out at the gates. Andromache cradles the head of "man-killing Hector" and grieves over his short life. She says that their city will be sacked, since Hector no longer protects them. She predicts that all Trojan women and children will be hauled away to labor for heartless masters. Her baby, she says, may be hurled down from the ramparts instead, when an enemy realizes he is Hector's son. Hector "was no man of mercy," she tells her son.

All the women wail, and Hecuba leads them in "a throbbing chant of sorrow." Helen says Hector was the dearest to her of all Paris' brothers and that she wishes she'd died before that fateful day that she came to Troy twenty years earlier. She says that always Hector was kind to her and stood up for her. While earlier Andromache described Hector as a man of no mercy, here he is clearly described as merciful, but, curiously, by a woman who is from what is now the enemy camp. She, too, explains how horrid her life will now be without Hector. Her lines are the final quoted words of sorrow.

The men collect timber for nine days, and then on the tenth they light the pyre, collect Hector's bones, set them in a golden chest, and hastily bury it, in case the Argives attack earlier than promised. The Trojans share "a splendid funeral feast" in Priam's house, "king by will of Zeus," we are reminded.

Critical Views

C.M. BOWRA ON THE CHARACTERS

Homer's real creative successes with Troy are of quite a different character. In the Achaean camp he created his galaxy of warriors. In Troy he creates women, the old man Priam, and the cause of all the trouble, Paris. Clearly he is right. In this assembly we get the life of the beleaguered city, the life which Hector is fighting to defend. Paris is the connecting link between the Trojan soldiers and the civilians. His character is drawn with such mastery that it is surprising that it has been so often misunderstood. He is not, as has been said, a coward. He is captain of a great host of Trojans (M 93), Aeneas believes in him (N 490), and Hector believes in him (N 766). On the third day of fighting his skill saves the Trojans from disaster (Λ 504 ff). It is true that he is an archer and open to some charge of being unsporting, but he is quite willing to put on armour when he is called to do so and to fight a duel with the redoubtable Menelaus. Nor would the Trojans respect him if he were a coward, and that they certainly do. For in the council where Antenor suggests that Helen should be returned to Menelaus, the refusal of Paris is enough to get the proposal rejected at once (H 357 ff.). But he is vain and rather frivolous. Hector treats him for what he is worth, and sends him to battle with a few harsh words. Paris bears him no resentment for this and goes to battle gladly (Γ 59, Z 333) His emptiness comes out most in the moving scene with Helen, where he does not understand that she is tired of him, and insists on his rights over her. He is frivolous and sensual, and therefore Hector rather despises him. But he has superficial grace and charm, and some animal qualities of gaiety and courage. He is not good enough for Helen, and part of her tragedy is that she knows it.

Priam is the old man who has learned not to expect too much out of life but to take things as they come. His faculties are still alert, and he inquires with insight into the personalities of the Achaean heroes, and thinks how far greater their army is than any he saw as a boy. He is the antithesis of Nestor, for whom nothing is as good as it once was. He has lost his illusions, and the loss has left him gentle. He has only words of kindness and comfort for Helen, and he bears with resignation the loss of most of his sons. But he nurses one dear hope in Hector, and his tragedy is that he loses even this.

(...)

The list of these important characters does not exhaust the wonders of Homer's creation. Even quite unimportant persons are brought by some magic touch to a sudden and short-lived vitality. Thersites, with his physical deformities and his flow of rancorous speech, Dolon, the only son with five sisters (*K* 317), Briseis, who loses her only friend in Patroclus (*T* 287 ff.)—all these come to life in their small parts, and there are others who come at once to mind for some passionate moment or heroic gesture, Asius driving recklessly across the Achaean trench (*M* 100 ff.), or old Chryses calling on Apollo in his despair (*A* 37 ff.). The *Iliad* is full of real beings, and Homer's creation never fails. There are many characters, but they never lack reality, and no character is the pale shadow of another. Homer's task was a hard one. The circumstances of war are not the easiest for the creation of a wide range of different characters, but he met the difficulty by setting his picture of war against a background of home life in Troy, and creating a world of women and old men to contrast with the heroism and cruelty of war. He was tied, too, by the convention of his time that his characters must be heroic, and though he keeps the convention, they are still alive. He is largely helped in this by the unexampled richness of his language, but they might easily have sunk sometimes from the heroic level. Only those whom he despises, Thersites and poor Dolon, are below standard, and they are so created intentionally. The heroes are always heroic in their language, their bravery, their amazing vitality. But unlike many heroes, they never lose their humanity. By selecting the essential characteristics and stressing them, Homer makes his personalities real. They may lack the complication or the subtlety possible in drama or the novel, but they have always outline and clarity, and their actions come from themselves. In the strict limits of the epic story there is no place for irrelevance. The character must hit the mark at once, or it is a failure. The outline must be clear, the poet cannot afford to blur the edges. Otherwise the characters would be too like each other and there would be no essential difference between Achilles and Diomedes.

MILMAN PARRY ON THE TRADITIONAL METAPHOR IN HOMER

So even the one active metaphor of the first *Iliad*—and the rest of Homer is in no way different—fails to do what Aristotle said the metaphor must do—that is, show why Homer was like no other poet.

At least, it fails to do so in the way that Aristotle meant, for really these metaphors that have been emptied of their meaning do show just what the natural talent of Homer was: it was a talent that worked not in the new but in the traditional. A careless reader of the foregoing pages may have thought that each one of the fixed metaphors which had lost its force was so much to be counted against Homer, but the example of fixed diction in English poetry should have shown him that what the words and phrases lost in meaning they had gained in kind of charm which pleased the poet and his hearers. As the fixed diction of the Augustan age can only be understood as the expression of a whole way of life which we may call the proper, so Homer's traditional diction is the work of a way of life which we may call the heroic, if one will give that word all the meaning it had for the men of Homer's time. It is a term which can only be understood in the measure that one can think and feel as they did, for the heroic was to them no more or less than the statement of all that they would be or would do if they could. To give form to this heroic cast of thought they had the old tales that had come down in time, and they had a rhythm in which to tell them, and words and phrases with which to tell them. The making of this diction was due to countless poets and to many generations who in time had found the heroic word and phrase for every thought, and every word in it was holy and sweet and wondrous, and no one would think of changing it wilfully. The Muses it was truly who gave those poets voices sweeter than honey. And those parts of the diction which did not carry the story itself, since their meaning was not needed for understanding, lost that meaning, but became, as it were, a familiar music of which the mind is pleasantly aware, but which it knows so well that it makes no effort to follow it. Indeed, poetry thus approaches music most closely when the words have rather a mood than a meaning. Nor should one think that since the meaning is largely lost it ceases to matter if the meaning is good. Though the meaning be felt rather than understood it is there, as it matters whether music idly heard be bad or good. Of such a kind is the charm of the fixed metaphor in Horner. It is an incantation of the heroic.

Aristotle did not understand this. Between the final vanishing of the old oral poetry and his own time two hundred years or more had already passed, and, thinking of Homer as he thought of the epic poetry of his own age, he failed to see that the metaphor was one thing for Antimachus and another for Homer. Modern critics, on the other hand, whose study was more careful, have found that Homer used the metaphor quite otherwise than Aristotle thought, and we ourselves have seen how utterly right they are, so that we are forced to choose between Aristotle's view of the nature of metaphor, in which case we must condemn Homer as mere copier, and the view that a traditional poet is good not because of the new that he brings into verse but because he knows how to make use of the traditional. If we do this we have found a charm far beyond any which can be found by men who wilfully wish to read Homer as they would any poetry of their own day. Indeed, the Greeks were not the men to carry the historical method of criticism to any such point. For that there had to come a new world which did not know the old by birthright but which, seeking rules of art for itself in times past reasoned much about that art, and more and more closely. In literary criticism generally this was the growth of the historical spirit. In Homeric criticism it was first the growing scorn for Homer's art in the sixteenth and seventeenth and eighteenth centuries in Italy, France, and England; then the period of Wolf and his followers who, however much they may have failed to grasp the meaning of what they did find, left no doubt that the *Iliad* and *Odyssey* were not such poems as we would ever write, or as Virgil and Dante and Milton wrote; and lastly of our own days in which, through a study of the oral poetries of peoples outside our own civilization, we have grasped the idea of traditional poetry. There is not a verse in Homer that does not become clearer and greater when we have understood that he too was a traditional poet. This way lies all true criticism and liking of his poems.

Erich Auerbach on Odysseus' Scar

As a composition, the old Testament is incomparably less unified than the Homeric poems, it is more obviously pieced together—but the various components all belong to one concept of universal history and its interpretation. If certain elements survived which did not immediately fit in, interpretation took care of them; and so the reader is at every moment aware of the universal religio-historical perspective which gives the individual stories their general meaning and purpose. The greater the separateness and horizontal disconnection of the stories and groups of stories in relation to one another, compared with the *Iliad* and the *Odyssey*, the stronger is their general vertical connection, which holds them all together and which is entirely lacking in Homer. Each of the great figures of the Old Testament, from Adam to the prophets, embodies a moment of this vertical connection. God chose and formed these men to the end of embodying his essence and will—yet choice and formation do not coincide, for the latter proceeds gradually, historically, during the earthly life of him upon whom the choice has fallen. How the process is accomplished, what terrible trials such a formation inflicts, can be seen from our story of Abraham's sacrifice. Herein lies the reason why the great figures of the Old Testament are so much more fully developed, so much more fraught with their own biographical past, so much more distinct as individuals, than are the Homeric heroes. Achilles and Odysseus are splendidly described in many well-ordered words, epithets cling to them, their emotions are constantly displayed in their words and deeds—but they have no development, and their life-histories are clearly set forth once and for all. So little are the Homeric heroes presented as developing or having developed, that most of them—Nestor, Agamemnon, Achilles—appear to be of an age fixed from the very first. Even Odysseus, in whose case the long lapse of time and the many events which occurred offer so much opportunity for biographical development, shows almost nothing of it. Odysseus on his return is exactly the same as he was when he left Ithaca two decades earlier. But what a road, what a fate, lie between the Jacob who cheated his father out of his blessing and the old man whose favorite son has been torn to pieces by a wild beast!—between David the harp player, persecuted by his lord's jealousy, and the old king, surrounded by violent intrigues, whom Abishag the Shunnamite warmed in his bed, and he knew her not! The old man, of whom we know how he has become what he is, is more of an individual than the young man; for it is only during the course of an eventful life that men are differentiated into full individuality; and it is this history of a personality which the Old Testament presents to us as the formation undergone by those whom God has chosen to be examples. Fraught with their development, sometimes even aged to the verge of dissolution, they show a distinct stamp of individuality entirely foreign to the Homeric heroes.

(...)

We have compared these two texts, and, with them, the two

kinds of style they embody, in order to reach a starting point for an investigation into the literary representation of reality in European culture. The two styles, in their opposition, represent basic types: on the one hand fully externalized description, uniform illumination, uninterrupted connection, free expression, all events in the foreground, displaying unmistakable meanings, few elements of historical development and of psychological perspective; on the other hand, certain parts brought into high relief, others left obscure, abruptness, suggestive influence of the unexpressed, "background" quality, multiplicity of meanings and the need for interpretation, universal-historical claims, development of the concept of the historically becoming, and preoccupation with the problematic.

Homer's realism is, of course, not to be equated with classical-antique realism in general; for the separation of styles, which did not develop until later, permitted no such leisurely and externalized description of everyday happenings; in tragedy especially there was no room for it; furthermore, Greek culture very soon encountered the phenomena of historical becoming and of the "multilayeredness" of the human problem, and dealt with there in its fashion; in Roman realism, finally, new and native concepts are added. We shall go into these later changes in the antique representation of reality when the occasion arises; on the whole, despite them, the basic tendencies of the Homeric style, which we have attempted to work out, remained effective and determinant down into late antiquity.

M.I. FINLEY ON MORALS AND VALUES

It is in the nature of honour that it must be exclusive, or at least hierarchic. When everyone attains equal honour, then there is no honour for anyone. Of necessity, therefore, the world of Odysseus was fiercely competitive, as each hero strove to outdo the others. And because the heroes were warriors, competition was fiercest where the highest honour was to be won, in individual combat on the field of battle. There a hero's ultimate worth, the meaning of his life, received its final test in three parts: whom he fought, how he fought, and how he fared. Hence, as Thorstein Veblen phrased it, under 'this commonsense barbarian appreciation of worth or honour, the taking of life ... is honourable in the highest degree. And this high office of slaughter, as an expression of the slayer's prepotence, casts a glamour of worth over every act of slaughter and over all the tools and accessories of the act.'[1] The *Iliad* in particular is saturated in blood, a fact which cannot be hidden or argued away, twist the evidence as one may in a vain attempt to fit archaic Greek values to a more gentle code of ethics. The poet and his audience lingered lovingly over every act of slaughter: 'Hippolochus darted away, and him too he [Agamemnon] smote to the ground; slicing off his hands with the sword and cutting off his neck, he sent him rolling like a round log through the battle-throng' (XI 145–7).

To Nietzsche the constant repetition of such scenes and their popularity throughout the Greek world for centuries to come demonstrated that 'the Greeks, the most humane men of ancient times, have a trait of cruelty, a tigerish lust to annihilate'.[2] But what must be stressed about Homeric cruelty is its heroic quality, not its specifically Greek character. In the final analysis, how can prepotence be determined except by repeated demonstrations of success? And the one indisputable measure of success is a trophy. While a battle is raging only the poet can observe Agamemnon's feat of converting Hippolochus into a rolling log. The other heroes are too busy pursuing glory for themselves. But a trophy is lasting evidence, to be displayed at all appropriate occasions. Among more primitive peoples the victim's head served that honorific purpose; in Homer's Greece armour replaced heads. That is why time after time, even at great personal peril, the heroes paused from their fighting in order to strip a slain opponent of his armour. In terms of the battle itself such a procedure was worse than absurd, it might jeopardize the whole expedition. It is a mistake in our judgement, however, to see the end of the battle as the goal, for victory without honour was unacceptable; there could be no honour without public proclamation, and there could be no publicity without the evidence of a trophy.

In different ways this pattern of honour-contest-trophy reappeared in every activity. Achilles could find no more fitting way to mourn his dead comrade than to set up a competitive situation in which the Achaean nobles might display their athletic prowess. The moment Diomedes brought his chariot to the finishing line in first place he leaped to the ground and 'he lost no time; ... eagerly he took the prize and gave his high-spirited companions the woman to lead away and the tripod with handles to carry; and he unyoked the horses' (XXIII 510–13). This unselfconscious delight in the prizes, demonstrated before the excited assemblage, had little to do with their intrinsic worth; Diomedes, like Achilles, had slave women and tripods enough in his hut. His impetuosity—he did not even stop to attend to his horses—was an emotional response, open and unabashed, honour triumphant. We might call it a boyish gesture; for Diomedes it was pride in his manliness.

Notes

1. *The Theory of the Leisure Class* (New York: Modern Library, 1934; London: Allen & Unwin, 1924), p. 18.

2. *Homer's Contest*, in *The Portable Nietzsche*, translated and edited by Walter Kaufmann (New York: Viking, 1954; London: Chatto & Windus, 1970, p. 32.

ALBIN LESKY ON THE *ILIAD'S* MATERIALS AND COMPOSITION

The architectonic grandeur of this plan has never been more truly appreciated than it was by Aristotle. In the *Poetics* (23. 1459a30, cf. 26. 1462b10) he contrasts the genius of its plan with the cyclic epics: Homer does not recount the whole history of the war—he selects one part and enlivens it with numerous episodes. We may add that these episodes meet Aristotle's requirement of being pertinent (οἰκέια 17.1455b13): the single exception, the *Doloneia*, will be discussed later. We can make Aristotle more explicit: the central conception, that of assembling and articulating a series of events around the theme of Achilles' anger, is realized in such a way as to turn the narration into a 'tale of Troy' at the same time. The duration of the action has been reckoned as fifty days; but if we deduct intervals of inactivity such as the nine days' plague, the twelve days in which the gods are with the Ethiopians, the twelve days of insulting Hector's body, there remain only a few days which receive detailed narrative treatment. In this short compass Homer contrives to mirror the entire war against Troy. He does so by two methods. The brief narrative of the quarrel is followed by more spaciously managed scenes of the Trojan war. Among these is the sounding of opinion in the army—a scene which would be strange out of its context, but makes good sense where it is: nine years have passed, the Greeks are war-weary, and new efforts are needed to set the siege in train once more. This start of a new phase enables the poet to bring in elements which would normally belong to the opening of the war—the *teichoscopia* and the proposal to settle the issue by single combat.

On the other hand Homer uses forward-looking references, scattered throughout the poem, which make the tragic issue of the action a characteristic element in the narrative. He does this both for Achilles and for the Trojan people—the principal actors in the drama—without any narration in the poet's own words. Under the impact of Pandarus' treachery, Agamemnon speaks confidently of the city's downfall (4. 164): on Hector's lips (6. 448) the same words seem the expression of a gloomy certainty. Diomedes also, on hearing the proposal to meet half the Greek demands, cries out that any simpleton can see that the Trojans are in the toils of destruction (7. 401). This kind of anticipation comes more often in the latter half of the poem,[1] and we so completely identify the Trojan resistance with Hector that his end seems the end of the city. Achilles stands in the shadow of early death from the very first conversation with his mother (1. 416); and from passage to passage the threat of his death is ever more sharp and definite.[2]

Thus through all the various episodes of this great poem interest is concentrated on a few leading themes and on a few leading actors. On these Homer bestows that strongly marked personality which the Greeks called 'ethos'. The shape that he gave to the characters earned the praise of Aristotle (*Poet.* 24. 1460a10) and became the norm in Greek poetry and the whole western literary tradition.

Three of them receive from the poet a destiny with strong tragic colouring. Achilles[3] in particular treads the path of his own uncontrollable passions. The decisive hour comes for him when the three ambassadors beg him to alter his decision. He himself declares (9. 645) that his judgment is not master of his resentment: and in consequence he has to lose his best friend and hasten his own death by taking revenge on Hector. He is depicted as not without insight. It would be wrong to speak of repentance; but the speaker does show awareness of the fatal interconnection when he tells Thetis (18. 98 ff.) that all his prowess has done is to spread misery around him, and he curses strife and anger which darken men's counsel. The swine theme is alluded to in his words to Agamemnon where they are first reconciled (19. 56). Hector[4] is driven by his success to overstep the bounds marked out for him. He hears Polydamas' threefold warning, yet goes his way to his own death and the ruin of those whom he loves. A passage of book 17 justifies us in using the word 'tragic': Zeus looks down at Hector, putting on Achilles' armour which he has won; he pities the poor mortal as he delights in his splendid equipment while the gates of death open before him. In his soliloquy before the Scacan gate, when he expects to die by his enemy's hand (22. 99), he also has his moment of insight: he sees that he has been wrong, and significantly enough Polydamas and his warnings come back to his mind. Equally so Patroclus knows no restraint in victory; his friends too warned him in vain, and he paid for it with his life.

The kind of destiny allotted to these three personages invites comparison with tragedy, and the comparison is important if

74

we are properly to appreciate the *Iliad*. The poem does not merely fulfil the demands of epic poetry: it goes far beyond them towards the realm of tragedy. Instead of uniform flow and unhurried narration of events, we find an artistic scheme of interconnection and cross-reference, happenings sometimes briefly sketched, sometimes elaborately worked out. This applies to the main themes. Many sections, however—blow-by-blow narratives of battles, standard scenes and descriptions, etc.—belong to the ordinary stock of epic. Aristotle (*Rhet.* 3, 9. 1409a24) divides style into two main classes—the flowing and the periodic. We may apply this conception to the construction of the *Iliad*: a structure of elaborate artistry contains considerable stretches of simple, flowing epic narrative.

Notes

1. W. Schadewaldt, *Iliasstudien*. Leipz. 1938, 156, 4.

2. *Iliad* 1, 416. 18, 95. 19. 408, 416. 21, 110. 22, 358.

3. Luciana Quaglia, 'La figura di Achille e l'etica dell' Iliade'. *Atti della Accad. Belle Scienze di Torino* 95, 1960/61.

4. E. Wüst, 'Hektor und Polydamas'. *Rhein. Mus.* 98, 1955, 335. Luciana Quaglia, 'La figura di Ettore e l'etica dell' Iliade'. *Atti della Accad. delle Scienze di Torino* 94, 1959/60.

CEDRIC H. WHITMAN ON HOMERIC CHARACTER AND THE TRADITION

In scene after scene, the character of Agamemnon, which one might a priori expect to be massive and imposing, is undercut with consistency throughout the poem. Yet the touch is everywhere light, and Agamemnon is allowed to gain sympathy, if not respect. His very weakness, the helpless way he stumbles against his own limits and infinite pretensions, win him some measure of compassion. He usually offends those whom he addresses, except his immediate henchmen, who suppress their feelings.[35] A little scene with Teucer is most characteristic; Teucer is doing well in battle, and wins Agamemnon's praise:

If ever Zeus the aegis-holder and Athena grant me
To spoil the well-founded citadel of Troy,
Into your hand I will put a token of honor,
First—after myself ...

Teucer impudently answers: "Why do you spur me on when I am working on my own account?"[36] and Agamemnon vanishes for the rest of the book. One of his best features is perhaps his solicitous care for Menelaus, yet this devotion is wholly unlike the high-hearted friendship of Diomedes and Sthenelus, the passionate unity of Achilles and Patroclus, or the studious and admiring love of Nestor for the gallant younger men. Agamemnon fusses over Menelaus and worries about him. When Menelaus is grazed by an arrow, Agamemnon's lament over the wound is almost hysterical.[37] No great warrior himself, Menelaus has a fine moment when he rises to answer Hector's challenge, and hopes the rest of the Achaeans turn to "earth and water," for being so spiritless; but Agamemnon seizes him and makes him sit down in safety.[38] His very solicitude betokens more fear than love, even as his prayer for the army's safety, by contrast with the famous prayer of Ajax for death under a clear sky, accents his timorous nature. insecure in itself and a fuse of alarm to others.[39]

(...)

With the first attempt to weld the short tales of single exploits into a panorama of all the heroes, a new problem arises. The characters must either duplicate each other to the point of utter boredom, or their individual differences must begin to distinguish them. Once the latter process has begun, we are on our way toward that extraordinary roster of unforgettable individuals which Homer presents. His formulation is surely not the only one which ever could have been, though its self-completeness suggests as much. Any bard dealing with the amalgamation of epic traditions must have attempted something of the sort. But Homer's construction is the one which impressed the Greeks, and laid the basis for all subsequent conceptions of the figures of myth, both gods and heroes, as Herodotus says.[42] But the process of distinguishing the characters of tradition involved more than merely letting the inevitable happen. It meant building consciously upon rudimentary data; it involved a shift of interest from merely what happened (to the greater glory of somebody) to how and why it happened, to whom, and through the agency of what sort of man. In the *Iliad*, at least, the question even arises as to what is the greater glory, and to whom can it come. It is naive to think that Homer celebrates all his heroes equally simply because his epithets do. The keen principle of dramatic selection is constantly at work in his exploration of the meaning of heroism. In Homer, many are called to the heroic trial, but in the last analysis, only one is chosen.

Notes

35. See the ἐπιπώλησις in Book IV, and note especially Diomedes' reply, 401–418; a passage taken rightly by Leaf to show that Diomedes, as ruler of Tiryns, was a vassal of Agamemnon.

36. VIII.287–294.

37. IV.155ff.

38. VII.96–119. One of the most cogent reasons for believing the *Doloneia* belongs somehow to Homer, and perhaps the *Iliad*, is the scene where Agamemnon deflects Diomedes from choosing Menelaus as a companion, 237ff.

39. Cf. VIII.236–244 with XVII.645ff.; see Longinus' remarks, *De Sublimitate*, IX.10.

42. Herod., II.53.2.

G.S. KIRK ON A RECONSIDERATION OF THE PLAIN STYLE

Both *Iliad* and *Odyssey* are full of people talking at length. In the sixteenth book of the former, for instance, nearly a third consists of direct speech. Nowhere in either poem are there long stretches of narrative undiversified by speech; it is striking, for example, how much utterance the poet has managed to inject into his version of the folktale adventures of Odysseus in distant lands. Virgil and Milton present a distinctly different picture. In the former, speeches are a relatively unimportant component; they may serve a directly rhetorical purpose (for example of exhortation or persuasion) or make a minimal concession to the realistic narration of human contacts, but the poet is clearly happiest when he is describing events, including personal exchanges, in his own words. In *Paradise Lost*, on the other hand, speech is crucial at particular points; book XI, for example, is for the most part composed of long interchanges between Adam and Eve, Eve and the serpent, Eve and herself, and with Adam again; and the two preceding books formally consist of conversations between Adam and Raphael. Yet elsewhere objective narrative predominates, so that it cannot be said that normal Miltonic practice has much in common with Homer's constant predilection for direct speech.

This predilection is certainly not an innovation by the monumental composer himself—although he may well have accentuated the practice as he probably did with the use and scale of similes. A relatively heavy speech-element must have formed part of the oral epic tradition in Greece for many generations; so much can be asserted for purely linguistic reasons, because of the organic presence of fully developed formulas in contexts exclusive to direct speech. But I would go further than that and suggest that the use of direct speech was probably an extremely ancient characteristic of the epic tradition in Greece. It is already marked in the *Epic of Gilgamesh* and was not inconspicuous in the Mesopotamian poetical style as a whole; and, without asserting direct imitation or many specific details in common, I remain convinced that narrative and poetical trends in second-millennium Greece, like mythological and religious ones, were strongly affected by the ancient Near East and in particular by Mesopotamia.

Yet Homer's use of speeches involves more than the maintenance of a literary tradition or the conventional form of a *genre*. It is through direct speech by the heroes that the poet expresses the heroic *ethos* that is, at the very least, an important part of his epic plan. He does not do so by direct exposition, or even primarily by the contriving of heroic situations, in themselves. Moreover he refrains from comment in his own person and keeps subjective judgements virtually out of his poetry. That is one possible result of a long oral tradition, although not a necessary one—the Yugoslav *guslari*, for instance, were not averse from personal comment. Yet in one way it is inevitable that Homer should reflect heroic attitudes through the words of his heroic characters. For much of the Homeric epic is essentially dramatic in conception, and in this respect it differs seriously from most of its successors. It presents the action as drama. That explains something important about the tendency to represent the interplay of persons through their own words, and has its own reasons.

First, most oral singers seem to share the ambition of the *guslari* to 'tell it as it really was'. When Odysseus wishes to praise the Phaeacian singer Demodocus describing the suffering of the Achaeans he does so by saying that Demodocus has sung the events 'in exceptionally good order', λίην ... κατὰ κόσμον. What better way to do this than by drawing out of the past the actual words, the threats and boasts and questionings, of the long-dead heroes themselves? Secondly, whereas Virgil is an interpreter, a *vates*, an artist who presents his audience with situations seen and understood through himself, the oral poet conceives himself rather as passively receiving his material from the past by the gift of the gods. He is mainly a receptacle (at least in his own estimation), and if he claims to be 'self-taught'[20] that refers only to the development of his particular repertory and means of embellishment. So Homer's allegiance to this kind of tradition keeps even his ambition relatively concrete: to recreate a real if vanished world rather than to divine the inner meaning of history or the destiny of men. Thirdly, the oral singer may have become temperamentally almost incapable of paraphrasing in his own words what a character was thinking or feeling. His natural method was to elicit the character's own expression of that. The idea of saying things like 'Achilles at this point was rejecting all the usual beliefs about warfare', or more simply 'he realized the whole endeavour was futile' seems not to have occurred, or to have been rejected as inappropriate. Simpler psychological descriptions like 'X wondered which of two courses to follow' are not uncommon, but when feelings become more complicated than that then X's own statement of those feelings becomes necessary. For the feelings are the man; the poet-reporter describes the man acting, and an important part of the action is the acting out of his thoughts and feelings through speech. It would detract from the realism of the description if the poet interposed himself as interpreter at this point. Acting, thinking, feeling, saying are interconnected aspects of the hero's involvement with his excessively codified environment.

Note
20. As Phemius does at *Odyssey* 24, 37.

JASPER GRIFFIN ON THE DIVINE AUDIENCE AND THE RELIGION OF THE *ILIAD*

It seems perhaps most natural to us to think of all this as being far more a matter of literature than of real religion; but the ancients thought of Homer as one of those who formed their theology. So it may be less bizarre than might at first sight appear, to point out that this aspect of the *Iliad* could be described in the words used of his own religion by so passionate a religious thinker as Pascal:

It is dangerous to let a man see too dearly how much he has in common with the animals, without at the same time making him realize his greatness. It is also dangerous to let him see his greatness too clearly, without realizing his baseness. It is more dangerous still to leave him in

80

ignorance of both. But it is very advantageous to draw attention to both.[66]

Both the baseness and the greatness of man are vital to the *Iliad*, and they are brought out with equal force and emphasis. The poet could say of his poem what Pascal says of his own work: 'If man exalts himself, I abase him; if he abases himself, I exalt him.' Pascal means that men are like animals because of sin and the Fall, Homer that they are like leaves because of their insignificance and lack of divinity; that is a difference which it would be flippant to minimize. But I think the comparison helps to show that the Iliadic presentation is compatible with a view of the world and human life which is both tragic and truly religious. If the poem did not rest on such a view, one both universal and serious, it could hardly be the great and profound work which it is.

That the gods, especially Zeus, observed human actions, was a natural and universal idea. That they contemplated them as a moving but also entertaining spectacle was not; and the gods had to pay a certain price for the great benefits it gave the poem in literary terms. Already in Homer it is at moments on the point of becoming a reproach to them that they 'look on' at injustice or suffering; but that is another story. It remains here to consider the sort of effects made possible by the Iliadic conception. Sometimes dramatic, sometimes small and inconspicuous, they are of great importance for the poem.

We have already discussed the opening of *Iliad* 13, Zeus turning away his shining eyes and leaving men to their unending labour and pain. Similar is the contrast, all the more effective for being unstressed, in a passage like this, of the partisanship of Zeus and Poseidon for the two warring sides:

'Those two mighty sons of Cronos, their wills in conflict, were contriving pain and suffering for heroic men.'

In the eleventh book Zeus 'stretched the lines of battle level, gazing down from Mount Ida, and they slaughtered each other'

(11.336). Apollo destroys the Achaean wall as a child destroys a sand-castle:

> 'So did you, Phoebus, shatter much labour and sweat of the Argives ... '[67]

Again, Zeus sits by himself, ignoring the hostility of the other gods,

> 'Gazing on the city of Troy and the Achaean ships, and the flash of bronze, and men slaying and being slain'.

Such details bring out the full complexity of human and divine action and suffering: the frightful impact on men of the intervention of immeasurably superior gods. For men, suffering, labour, and death; for the gods, serene observation and easy action. We have seen this again in passages which bring out the difference between a man who is 'god-like' and a real god.[68]

These passages derive their power from the existence of the divine audience. The gods look on, and under their shining gaze human achievements and human suffering are seen in a certain unique way. We are able to share their viewpoint and to see human life as they see it, in its double aspect of greatness and littleness. And the gods themselves acquire not least from their role of watchers their own complex nature: sublime heavenly witnesses and judges, and at the same time all-too-human spectators and partisans. The development of the real and simple religious conception into a complex literary device was momentous for the later literature and religion of antiquity.

Notes

66. Blaise Pascal, *Pensées*, ed. Pléiade, 1170: 'Il est dangereux de trop faire voir à l'homme combien il est égal aux bêtes, sans lui montrer sa grandeur. Il est encore dangereux de lui trop faire voir sa grandeur sans sa bassesse. Il est encore plus dangereux de lui laisser ignorer l'un et l'autre. Mais il est très avantageux de lui représenter

l'un et l'autre.' Trans. M. Turnell (1962). And again: 'Si l'homme se vante, je l'abaisse; s'il s'abaisse, je le vante.'

67. Cf. 12.29, the eventual complete effacement by the gods of the wall, 'which the Achaeans toiled to build'.

68. Pp. 83 ff. above.

SETH L. SCHEIN
ON HECTOR AND TROY

Hektor and Achilles appear or are referred to more frequently than any other figures in the *Iliad*, Hektor in all twenty-four books and Achilles in every book except Book 3.[28] Their actions are the main actions of the poem, which reaches its climax when one kills the other. They speak at greater length and more vividly and individualistically than any other characters.[29] In this way they are characterized more deeply and fully, and their behavior is made to reflect the inner "selves" expressed by their speeches. The similes in which they are compared to elements of nature represent them as victor and victim respectively. Achilles, more often than any other hero, is compared to a predatory animal on the attack: for example, a lion (20.164–75, 24.41–45), a "great-gaping dolphin" (21.22–26), a hawk (22.139–42), and a dog chasing a fawn (22.189–90). Hektor never is compared to a predator, but instead several times is a predator's potential victim: for example, a dog chasing a lion or wild boar (8.338–42), a timid dove (22.140–42), and a fawn (22.189–92).

(...)

Like the boulder, Hektor rushes forward destructively until his force is spent and, in the end, lies motionless on the plain. Achilles, on the other hand, never is compared to a passive element of nature; he is, rather, like a raging forest fire (20.490–94) or the fever-bearing dog-star (22.26–32).

Perhaps the main difference between the two heroes is that Hektor is represented as quintessentially social and human, while Achilles is inhumanly isolated and daemonic in his greatness. This difference is reflected in numerous details throughout the poem. Achilles is cut off from his parents, who dwell far off in the depths of the sea and back home in Phthia, but Hektor's parents are present and watch him from the walls. While Achilles' mother sends her son into battle and to his death, when he wishes to go, and obtains new armor for him, Hecuba and Priam try to keep Hektor out of battle in order to save his life. Even Hektor's horses evoke a picture of his and Andromache's domestic life and its contradictory relation to his heroism: he reminds them that Andromache herself gives them honey-sweet grain to feed on and mixes wine for them to drink when they wish, even before she feeds "me, who claim to be her blooming husband" (8.190); therefore they ought to repay this care by helping him win greater glory (8.186, 191–97). On the other hand, Achilles' horses, immortal, serve chiefly to emphasize Achilles' unique closeness to the gods and therefore, by contrast, his doomed mortality: Zeus wonders whether the gods gave them as a wedding present to Peleus so that they must experience the griefs of wretched mortals (17.443–45), and one of them uncannily speaks to Achilles to prophesy his imminent death (19.408–17).

Achilles' closeness to the gods contributes to his isolation from his fellow humans; Hektor's family is part of what makes him paradigmatically human. For Achilles, the main thing in life is winning honor and glory; his disillusionment and attendant alienation in Book 9, and the isolated detachment he shares with Priam in Book 24, move him to his deepest perceptions about human existence. Hektor, preeminently a familial and social hero, whose sense of shame is his main heroic virtue, is led to his deepest perceptions by the reunion with his family in Book 6.

More important than the great differences between Hektor and Achilles is the final, elemental similarity between them: both are mortal, and both move in the course of the poem inescapably toward their deaths, helpless to understand fully or to alter the tragic circumstances of their existence. Achilles knows, and the audience or reader knows, from the beginning of the *Iliad* that he is "short-lived" (1.352) and "most swiftly-doomed beyond others" (1.505). This knowledge, objective and accurate as imparted by his divine mother, Achilles confirms in Book 18 by his decision to die at once provided that he can avenge the death of Patroklos. From that point on, references to his death increase and are intensified until by the end of the poem he is virtually dead. A similar fatality shadows Hektor from the end of Book 6 onward.

(...)

Even as Andromache is arousing in her servants the lament for Hektor, he is speaking to Paris about the possibility that

> ... Zeus
> may grant that for the heavenly gods who live forever
> we set up in our halls the mixing bowl of freedom,
> when we have driven the well-greaved Achaians from Troy.
>
> (6.526–29)

Even when Patroklos in his dying breath prophesies Hektor's death in the near future at the hands of Achilles (16.853–54), Hektor continues vainly to hope against hope:

> who knows if Achilles, the son of fair-haired Thetis,
> may first lose his life, having been hit by my spear?
>
> (16.860–61)

By contrast, Achilles readily accepts the death foretold to him by the dying Hektor, whenever it may come (22.358–66).

Hektor's inability to foresee his imminent death is but one facet of his generally limited perception of himself and his circumstances. He is trapped not only by these circumstances, that is, by the external conditions of his existence, but by his own character and his limited vision of reality.

Notes
28. A. Scott, *The Unity of Homer* (Berkeley, 1921), p. 218.
29. E. Bassett, *The Poetry of Homer* (Berkeley and Los Angeles, 1938), p. 78, notes that Hektor speaks more, and more picturesquely, than any other character except Achilles.

MARK W. EDWARDS ON SYMBOLISM

The same kinds of symbolism are often found in Homer, and Part Two draws attention to the major examples. Some are limited to a single scene: Hector's infant son squalls at the sight of his father's warrior helmet, and the doomed man lays it aside while he takes up the child and prays for a glorious future for him (6.466ff.; see p. 211). Achilles, wondering whether to kill Agamemnon there and then, half draws his sword, and thrusts it back into the sheath when he decides against such a rash act; a little later he dashes to the ground in disgust the staff held by the speaker in the assembly, the staff that symbolizes the civilized norms of behavior that have now fallen in ruins (1.188ff.; 245ff.: see pp. 180 and 181). Just before Patroclus's death, the helmet he is wearing, Achilles' own, made by a god, falls from his head and rolls in the dust, and the poet's own voice speaks of the event as a sign both of the disgrace his friend's death brings to Achilles and of the transient nature of Zeus' favor to Hector (see p. 264.

(...)

Such clear uses of symbolism suggest that the same technique should be recognized in the motif of Achilles' divinely made armor, which is important in many scenes in Books 16 to 22. The disguise of Patroclus in the armor given to Achilles by Peleus is hardly employed at all by the poet for any practical use (see p. 255), except that the loss of the armor when Patroclus is killed provides a convenient reason for Achilles' not entering battle immediately to seek vengeance, and of course leads up to the magnificent description of Hephaestus's making the new shield. But this divine armor was the gift of the gods to Achilles' human father, Peleus, at his marriage to the goddess Thetis, and by its very existence suggests the great gulf between mortals and immortals, not satisfactorily bridged by this short-lived and not very fruitful union; and Hephaestus's making the new armor in Book 18 is juxtaposed to Achilles' decision to seek vengeance even at the cost of his own death (see p. 269). So the old and new sets of armor constantly function as symbols of the contrast of mortals and gods, form a visible link between the deaths of Patroclus, Hector, and Achilles, and bring out the irony that the invulnerable armor cannot preserve the life of any of the three who wear it in the *Iliad* (see pp. 264 and 296).

When Patroclus puts on the armor, it identifies him as Achilles' surrogate in battle and in death (since Achilles will not die in the *Iliad*), and acts as a symbol of the concession Achilles is making to the Greeks. When Hector puts it on after it has been stripped from the dead Patroclus, his action shows arrogance and *hubris* (for Hector has no divine parent), and Zeus comments explicitly upon this: "Poor fool! death is not in your mind,/but it is close beside you; you put on the immortal armor/of a great man .../whose companion you have killed .../ and his armor improperly from his head and shoulders/you have taken" (17.201–6).

At the final duel, the armor Hector wears is the visible sign not only that he killed Patroclus, but that Achilles himself sent him to battle wearing it; we feel that Achilles' guilt intensifies his longing for revenge. There is even more than this; for Achilles accepted that his killing Hector would bring his own death closer (see p. 273), and so when he sees Hector wearing the armor he recognizes as his own and kills him, he is symbolically (and to the eye of an observer) killing him*self*. The contrast between mortals and immortals is powerfully before our eyes, for both heroes in this final confrontation are wearing god-given armor, which did not save Patroclus in the past, does not save Hector now, and will not save Achilles in the future.

There is another different intensifying effect we should

note, a kind of symbolic anticipation by which the foreground action casts a huge shadow of events to come. Hector's parting from his wife and son in Book 6 must be seen in the larger context of his later death at Achilles' hands, his wife's enslavement at the sack of Troy, and his son's murder by the victorious Greeks, all of which are directly or obliquely referred to in the scene. In his grief at the death of Patroclus, Achilles lies in the dust with his head in his mother's hands, and the tableau strongly suggests his own death and funeral (see p. 271). The renunciation by Achilles and the other heroes of the simple happiness of everyday life is suggested by the depiction on the shield not of heroic scenes but of the ordinary, familiar Greek existence. Perhaps this representation of human life through art by the smith god suggests the poet's own recreation of the human condition (see p. 285).

BERNARD KNOX ON THE GODS AND HEROES

The gods are immortal; they are not subject to time. They have all the time in the world. And so they are not subject to change, to the change brought by age, to the change brought by learning from suffering and a realization of limitations. They will always be what they are now and have always been; they are all the same at the end of the *Iliad* as at the beginning. They do not change, do not learn. How could they? They are the personification of those mysterious forces which through their often violent interaction produce the harsh patterns of human life—the rise and fall of nations, the destructiveness of the earthquake, the terror of the flood, the horrors of the plague, but also the sweetness of passionate love, the intoxication of wine, the extra strength that surges through a warrior's limbs at the moment of danger.

As personalities (and that is how Homer and the Greeks always saw them), they are very different from one another, but they have, besides immortality, one other thing in common—a furious self-absorption. Each one is a separate force which, never questioning or examining the nature of its own existence, moves blindly, ferociously, to the affirmation of its will in action. The Homeric god recognizes no authority outside itself—except superior force. How are arguments settled in heaven? Like this; "Obey my orders," says Zeus to Hera,

> *"for fear the gods, however many Olympus holds.*
> *are powerless to protect you when I come*
> *to throttle you with my irresistible hands."* (1.681–83)

The other gods do not argue with Zeus, though they may try to trick him, as Hera does successfully (14.187–421), and he does not explain his will to them, he threatens and enforces. There are no moral questions involved, only the clash of wills, intent on manifesting their existence—whether by bringing Troy to destruction or by driving Helen back into bed with Paris, as in the strange scene where Aphrodite, in the shape of an old woman, acts the procuress. "Quickly—Paris is calling for you, come back home! / There he is in the bedroom, the bed with inlaid rings ..." (3.450–51). Helen recognizes the goddess and resists her temptation: "Maddening one, my Goddess, oh what now? / Lusting to lure me to my ruin yet again?" (3.460–61). "Lusting" is not too strong a word; the mating of male and female is Aphrodite's very existence; that is why she is so stubborn to procure it. And she flares up in anger:

> *"Don't provoke me—wretched, headstrong girl!*
> *Or in my immortal rage I may just toss you over,*
> *hate you as I adore you now—with a vengeance ..."*
>
> *So she threatened*
> *and Helen the daughter of mighty Zeus was terrified.*
> (3.480–86)

And well she might be. Helen has nothing but her beauty and the charm it casts on all men; without Aphrodite she would be nothing. And Aphrodite plays the same role on Olympus as on earth. She gives Hera, who wants to divert Zeus's attention from the battle so Poseidon can help the Achaeans,

> *the breastband,*
> *pierced and alluring, with every kind of enchantment*
> *woven through it ... There is the heat of Love,*
> *the pulsing rush of Longing, the lover's whisper,*
> *irresistible—madness to make the sanest man go mad.*
> (14.257–60)

Zeus in his sphere of power, Aphrodite in hers, are irresistible. To be a god is to be totally absorbed in the exercise of one's own power, the fulfillment of one's own nature, unchecked by any thought of others except as obstacles to be overcome; it is to be incapable of self-questioning or self-criticism. But there are human beings who are like this. Preeminent in their particular sphere of power, they impose their will on others with the confidence, the unquestioning certainty of their own right and worth that is characteristic of gods. Such people the Greeks called "heroes"; they recognized the fact that they transcended the norms of humanity by according them worship at their tombs after death. Heroes might be, usually were, violent, antisocial, destructive, but they offered an assurance that in some chosen vessels humanity is capable of superhuman greatness, that there are some human beings who can deny the imperatives which others obey in order to live.

The heroes are godlike in their passionate self-esteem. But they are not gods, not immortal. They are subject, like the rest of us, to failure, above all to the irremediable failure of death. And sooner or later, in suffering, in disaster, they come to realize their limits, accept mortality and establish (or reestablish) a human relationship with their fellowmen. This pattern, recurrent in the myths of the Greeks and later to be the model for some of the greatest Athenian tragedies, is first given artistic form in the *Iliad*.

JOACHIM LATACZ ON THE THEME OF THE WRATH OF ACHILLES

Numerous singers will have presented the Troy saga or segments of it to their listeners in this normal way of telling a tale. Homer chooses a different perspective. He begins his rendition of the saga thus:

Sing the wrath, goddess, of the son of Peleus, Akhilleus!

The theme here is not the city and the struggle for it. The theme is, moreover, no external event at all. It is rather a process that takes place within an individual: a wrath. The narrative begins then not with major elements. Instead, it is restricted to the small-scale and—as it seems—the private, within the soul of an individual hero in the Akhaian army: the son of Peleus, Akhilleus. This perspective then is unlike that of the "normal" beginning. It offers a "view from within": the narrative gradually proceeds step-by-step from an internal point to the external. It embraces ever enlarging areas until the whole finally comes into view.

It is doubtful whether the mere reversal of perspective, that is, the change from an external to an internal perspective, was entirely new to Homer's audience. The presentation of large sequences of events from an individual's point of view is a very common narrative technique (seen in the form of direct discourse even in narratives told from an external perspective). Thus, we cannot go so far as to attribute its invention to Homer. What may be new, however, is the consistent "deepening" of this perspective, the shift "to a deeper level" within the individual hero.

Indeed, the *Iliad* commences not with the whole person "Akhilleus" but with the designation of a state of mind—to wit, "wrath." Homer does not begin, "Sing, goddess, of how the son of Peleus, Akhilleus, once grew wrathful"; rather, precisely the *menis*, or wrath, itself becomes an agent: "Sing the wrath, goddess, that brought pain to the Akhaians, sent many heroes' souls on the way to Hades, and made them the spoils of scavenging dogs and birds of prey!" The state of mind, too, not just the person, is valued here: "the wrath, accursed wrath!" (such translations as "the destructive wrath" or "the ruinous wrath" do not convey the sense of the word *menis* in the original [Kirk 1985, 53]). The wrath "does" something, it is to blame for something and is for that reason accursed. We see here an announcement of the story not of a noble hero and his deeds but of the inner condition of a human being and its effects. The interest is not so much in what the man does but in what transpires within him (and forms the basis for his action). It has rightly been suggested that we are witnessing a process of "internalizing" and a tendency to "psychologize the facts of the saga" (Kullmann 1981, 26). This tendency pervades the *Iliad*. It shifts the mythical incident to a deeper, interior level; and insofar as it deepens, it also clarifies. The *Iliad* becomes an interpretation of the Troy saga. This is Homer's first innovation—an innovation in the *direction* of focus.

Constituting a second innovation is the manner in the *Iliad* of looking at things, one might even say of judging things. The wrath of a hero is accursed; it reveals itself not as a positive, praiseworthy thing but as a negative force:

> ... that brought infinite pain to the Akhaians
> and hurled many strong souls down to Hades—souls of
>   heroes! ...

In the world of epic poetry, the anger of heroes is normally directed against the enemy and spurs the heroes to momentous deeds. Here, the wrath of Akhilleus is directed toward his own people and causes the death of his own comrades. The vector of action is thus reversed. What should be directed outward as a strength is directed inward as a weakness. The heroic appears not in its customary brilliance but bedimmed, even ominous. This impression is intensified by a further movement toward the negative—the death of the heroes is not merely stated but portrayed in horrific terms:

... and left them [viz., the heroes' bodies] to be booty for dogs and a banquet for the birds....

(The Greek *dais* [banquet], which denotes not a quick snack but a formal common meal, conjures up the macabre image of a festive dinner of birds of prey.) For a man of standing in Homer's time nothing was more disturbing than the prospect of lying dead and unburied in an open field to serve as food for dogs and vultures. Later in the *Iliad*, truces are regularly concluded for the sole purpose of recovering corpses. Therefore, this repulsively graphic image of dogs and birds ripping pieces from corpses stands at the beginning of our *Iliad* by design. It sends this message: so shockingly did the wrath of Akhilleus affect his comrades!

It is hard to imagine that this was the usual perspective on the heroes of the glorious Trojan expedition. The song of the war fought by noble ancestors around the citadel of Troy begins here with a profoundly repugnant image, void of any human dignity. This could hardly have failed to impress the audience. Emotions were stirred. Certainly an ancient commentator on this passage was right to say, "the violent emotions that the *prooimion* triggers [in listeners] are quite exceptional" (BT scholia; see Griffin 1980, 118). Above all, indignation will have been aroused, indignation toward the responsible party—Akhilleus—and toward this "accursed wrath" of his. The audience's need for decorum was supplanted by revulsion—against perhaps not only the character but also his creator. From the author's point of view, this was an infallible method of building suspense.

ALBERT BATES LORD ON THE LANGUAGE OF ARMS AND ARMING

Finally there is the epithet for Agamemnon's shield, "covering the whole man, man-enclosing," which is found, in the genitive, three more times in the *Iliad* (2.389, 12.402, and

20.281).[25] It is not used in the *Odyssey*. This is an epithet that cannot ordinarily be used with anything except a shield. In 2.388–89, Agamemnon is urging the Argives back to have dinner and to prepare their weapons for fighting; for they will fight all day without respite until darkness comes:

> There will be a man's sweat on the shield-strap binding the breast to the shield hiding the man's shape, and the hand on the spear grow weary.

Agamemnon's speech ends the assembly in which the Argives are turned back from returning home after the incident of the baneful Dream, a noteworthy speech in an important, if puzzling, episode of the epic.

Where the words 'man-enclosing shield' occur in 12.402, we also find a significant episode. Sarpedon has just pulled down part of the battlements:

> And Sarpedon, grabbing in both ponderous hands the battlements, pulled, and the whole thing came away in his hands, and the rampart was stripped defenceless above. He had opened a pathway for many.

At this point, Ajax and Teucer attack him:

> Aias and Teukros aimed at him together, and Teukros hit him with an arrow in the shining belt that encircled his chest to hold the man-covering shield, but Zeus brushed the death spirits from his son, and would not let him be killed there beside the ships' sterns.

So Sarpedon is spared for the time being.

The final instance of ἀσπίδος ἀμφιβρότες (20.281) is in another striking scene, the encounter of Achilles with Aeneas. The role of the shield is dramatic. Achilles has cast the Pelian ash spear, which struck the outer rim of the shield where it was thinnest:

94

> The Pelian ash spear
> crashed clean through it there, and the shield cried
> out as it went through.

The reaction of Aeneas involves the shield:

> Aineias shrank down and held the shield away and
> above him in fright, and the spear went over his back
> and crashed its way to the ground, and fixed there,
> after tearing apart two circles of the man-covering shield.

Aeneas stands stock still and is overcome with emotion when
he sees how close the spear came to him. He picks up a huge
stone "which no two men could carry/such as men are now,
but by himself he lightly hefted it." Achilles would have
fended it of with his shield and dispatched Aeneas with his
sword, but Poseidon intervenes with the gods to save Aeneas.
Poseidon's ensuing conversation with Athena and Hera is
reminiscent of Zeus's with the same worthies over the case of
his son Sarpedon. As a result, Poseidon goes to the field of
action (20.321–27):

> There quickly he drifted a mist across the eyes of one
>   fighter,
> Achilleus, Peleus' son, and from the shield of Aineias
>   of the great heart pulled loose the strong bronze-headed
>   ash spear
> and laid it down again before the feet of Achilleus;
> but Aineias he lifted high from the ground, and slung him
>   through the air
> so that many ranks of fighting men, many ranks of horses,
> were overvaulted by Aineias, hurled by the god's hand.

Although the sparing of Aeneas by Poseidon, playing
Aphrodite's role, reminds one, and quite rightly, of the scene in
which Sarpedon is spared and inevitably, and more cogently, of
course, also of the major scene in which he is not spared, it is
not the noun-epithet combination ἀσπίδος ἀμηιβρότς that

makes the association. Yet, as was the case with θώρηˊκος πολυδαιδάλον 'intricately worked corselet', these noun-epithet combinations tend to occur in significant passages, some of which are multiforms of the same thematic material. How many of the scenes to which these epithets have led us involved sparing the life of an important figure in the heroic world!

We could continue in this vein and broaden our experience of arms and arming, investigating the epithets and other key words, observing them in their several and varied contexts, but we have examined enough to illustrate Homer's technique. Sound patterns have been shown to play a large role in the choice of the epithets and in the phrasing of the lines. We have seen that Homer has a group of basic lines for arming, which he supplements and modifies as the scene and action require. We saw also that there are apparently only four armings in which this basic group forms the nucleus: that of Agamemnon, the longest and most special (in which the shield finds its closest parallel in the *Shield of Heracles*, not in Achilles' shield); those of Achilles and Patroclus; and finally, and perhaps somewhat strangely, that of Paris. Notable are the otherworldly or divine connections in the major three, excluding Paris's. In spite of the basic lines, the armings of Achilles and Paris are distinct and reflect the character of their heroes. It is clear that epithets are not used mechanically; rather, particular noun-epithet combinations recur in observable patterns in passages crucial for the action of the poem. A study of the ambiance of these phrases reveals their discriminating use in related passages important for their human and often divine associations. Their repetition is not accidental but helps to emphasize key ideas. Repetition and ornamentation are surely meaningful elements in oral epic tradition.

Note

25. See Lorimer, *Homer and the Monuments* (London: Macmillan, 1950): "It [Agamemnon's shield] is described as ἀμπηˊιβρότε, 'coming

around both sides of a man', an epithet originally designed for the body-shield, both forms of which are seen on the monuments to have a deep curvature within which the figure of the warrior disappears. The adjective is inappropriate to the round shield, which is sometimes quite flat and which, because its rim lies on one plane, cannot envelop the bearer even when it is convex. ἀμφιβρότε, which is used only with ἀσπίρ and, apart from B 389, only in contexts which show that the shield in question is round ... must have acquired in epic the general meaning of 'man-protecting'; the fact that it occurs only four times in the vulgate suggests that in Homer's day it was almost obsolete" (189).

MAUREEN ALDEN ON THE SHIELD OF ACHILLES

On the shield the murderer making a public statement that he wants to pay full restitution reminds us of Agamemnon and his offer to restore Briseis to Achilles and provide compensation for slighting him. The murder victim's kinsman who refuses to accept anything reminds us of Achilles, who rejects the compensation offered by Agamemnon through the ambassadors: ten or twenty times as much would not be enough. Achilles wanted recompense for the whole outrage (*Il.* 9. 378–87), but it is hard to see what form this could take if, as he says there, no offer would be sufficient. The correspondence between the shield's depiction of a refusal to accept compensation, and Achilles' refusal to accept the compensation offered by Agamemnon through the ambassadors is reinforced by Ajax's criticism of Achilles for a similar refusal. Ajax argues that a man accepts compensation even for the murder of a brother or a child: the murderer remains in the community, having paid a great deal, and the kinsman of the dead man restrains his indignation and rage when he has received the blood money (*Il.* 9. 632–6).[27] The injury done to Achilles by Agamemnon is less serious than that done by the murderer to his victim's kin. Therefore, if compensation is acceptable even in cases of murder, it should, in Ajax's view, be acceptable to Achilles, whose grievance is not so acute. Achilles even agrees with Ajax on an objective level:

'everything you have said is after my own mind' (*Il.* 9. 645), but in practice he is overwhelmed by indignation at Agamemnon's behaviour towards him, and cannot act upon his own objective views. Achilles and Agamemnon remain at loggerheads when the offer of compensation has been made and rejected, but on the shield the situation does not remain deadlocked with the rejection of compensation. Instead the two men on the shield are both eager to obtain a verdict on their dispute from a judge, and approach the elders for this purpose.[28] A prize of two talents is offered to the one (of the elders) who offers the best verdict.[29] And that is where the description of the first city stops: we do not learn what the verdict is, or how the dispute is resolved, because the poet is not concerned to determine which of the parties to the dispute is justified. His interest is in their decision to take their dispute to the elders for arbitration: the scene is closed when the arbitration is set up. It is precisely in the early resort to arbitration that the scene on the shield departs significantly from the repetition of the elements of the quarrel between Achilles and Agamemnon. The other elements, (1) the commission of offence, (2) the offer of compensation, and (3) the rejection of the offer are common to both the main narrative[30] and the scene on the shield. The trial scene on the shield presents a way out of the impasse caused by the rejection of compensation in stark contrast to the deadlock of the main narrative. The scenes of rejoicing in the city which has recourse to the judgement of the elders in a case of rejection of compensation contrast strongly with the tragic events of the main narrative, where the elders (Nestor in book 1 and the ambassadors in book 9) urging Achilles to accept compensation are disregarded. The audience might well consider the association of ideas: acceptance of the views of the elders is associated with the rejoicing of a communal wedding on the shield, whereas in the main narrative of the *Iliad* Achilles' failure to accept the views of the elders is associated with the loss of what is most precious, with mourning and the funeral of Patroclus. So it is clear that the issue of compensation presented in the first city on the shield relates to the issue of compensation in the main narrative as presented in the embassy of book 9.

Notes

27. Ø. Andersen, 'Some Thoughts on the Shield of Achilles', *SO* 51 (1976): 15; R. Westbrook, 'The Trial Scene in the *Iliad*', *HSCP* 94 (1992): 70.

28. The γέροντες here are invited to δικάζειν as the ἡγήτορες ἠδὲ μέδοντες are to δικάζειν between Antilochus and Menelaus at *Il.* 23. 573–4.

29. The shield shows two talents lying *in the middle* (*Il.* 18. 507) of the circle of elders, to be given to the one who offers the best judgement. The gifts given by Agamemnon to Achilles when the two men are finally reconciled are also displayed *in the middle* (*Il.* 19. 249) of the assembly of Greeks before Agamemnon swears his oath of reconciliation. Agamemnon's gifts are compensation, and as such, do not correspond to the prize to be offered for the best judgement in the case on the shield, but the image of goods exchanged in the context of resolution of a dispute suggests a loose association between the two talents on the shield and Agamemnon's gifts of reconciliation.

30. (1) Agamemnon's appropriation of Briseis; (2) Agamemnon's offer of compensation through the embassy of book 9; (3) Achilles' rejection of the embassy.

MARGALIT FINKELBERG ON THE SOCIAL PERSPECTIVE IN THE *ILIAD*

There is little doubt that the *Iliad* originated in the cultural and political milieu of aristocratic chiefdoms which preceded the formation of the city-state. Contrary to the system of values established with the rise of the polis, according to which the distribution of honour should follow personal achievement, the distribution of honour in pre–city-state society corresponded to a person's social status, which was determined by superiority in birth and wealth. Nowhere is this shown more clearly than in the description of the athletic contests held by Achilles at Patroclus' tomb in *Iliad* 23. In the chariot race, Eumelus who lost the competition is offered the second prize because he is "the best", *aristos*, and Menelaus who came third is again offered the second prize on exactly the same grounds, while in the throwing of the spear Agamemnon receives the first prize without even participating in the contest, only because he is *aristos* and superior to all others.[36] "After all," Moses Finley wrote of Homeric society, "the basic values of the society were given, predetermined, and so were a man's place in the society and the privileges and duties that followed from his status".[37] No wonder, therefore, that the chief motivation behind the Homeric warriors' behaviour was the drive to meet the expectations that ensued from their status. Together with risking one's life in war, these expectations also embraced assistance to and the protection of those to whom the person was tied by the mutual obligations of military alliance, guest-friendship, or vassal relations.[38]

It is however highly symptomatic that the lack of social equality and insufficient recognition of personal merit which directly result from the aristocratic ethos prevailing in the *Iliad* are questioned in the body of the *Iliad* itself. This can be seen first of all in Homer's treatment of the central issue of the poem, the conflict between Achilles and Agamemnon. "I have sacked twelve of men's cities from my ships", Achilles says bitterly in *Iliad* 9, "and I claim eleven more by land across the fertile Troad. From all of these I took many fine treasures, and every time I brought them all and gave to Agamemnon son of Atreus: and every time, back there by the fast ships he had never left, he would take them in, share out a few, and keep the most for himself."[39] Homer makes Achilles question the view of honour as bestowed automatically, according to status and birth, and pose the claim of merit as against the claim of rank. "Stay at home or fight your hardest—your share will be the same. Coward and Hero are given equal honour", Achilles says elsewhere in the same speech. It is not surprising, therefore, that in his *Politics* Aristotle adduces these Homeric lines in support of the argument that the distribution of honour must be proportionate to one's contribution to the well-being of the community.[40]

But Homer's criticism of aristocratic values goes even further. The main conflict of the *Iliad* is the conflict of Honour. It was because of considerations of honour which went against the common interest that Agamemnon took Briseis from Achilles and it was, again, considerations of honour that caused Achilles to withdraw from participation in the Trojan campaign from the moment that his prize of honour, *geras*, was taken from him. The issue of honour is thus woven into the core of the *Iliad* plot. At the same time, it would be wrong to say that the poet of the *Iliad* sides unambiguously with the considerations of personal honour and prestige which move his heroes and the plot of his poem. As I have argued elsewhere, in his treatment of the theme of Achilles' wrath in *Iliad* 11, 16, and 18 Homer criticizes aristocratic individualism and its self-serving value of personal honour, *timê*, and re-interprets the inherited plot of the *Iliad* in the spirit of the city-state value of *aretê*, personal excellence which benefits the entire community.[41] When in *Iliad* 11 Nestor says that Achilles' abstention from participating in the war will result in that he "will be the only one to profit from his excellence (οἶος τῆς αρετῆς απονήσεται)", or when in *Iliad* 16 Patroclus asks Achilles "what will any other man, even yet to be born, profit from you (τί σευ ἄλλος ὀνήσεται ὀφίγονός περ), if you do not save the Argives from shameful destruction?", and, finally, when in *Iliad* 18 Achilles himself comes to the conclusion that his chosen line of behaviour has resulted in that, instead of being "a saving light to Patroclus or many other companions", he has become "a useless burden on the earth", the concept underlying all these utterances is that by keeping his excellence, *aretê*, to himself Achilles has actually invalidated it and thus almost annihilated his own worth as "the best of the Achaeans".[42]

There can be no doubt that this was not the message which originally informed the poem. Consider again Achilles' words of self-reproach in *Iliad* 18: "I have not been a saving light to Patroclus or my many other companions who have been brought down by godlike Hector, but sit here by the ships, a useless burden on the earth." Whereas Achilles' obligations to

Patroclus, Achilles' "own" man, are among those values which are seen in terms of the aristocratic code of honour, the very design of the *Iliad* shows that no such terms could originally have been applied to Achilles' attitude to the rest of the Greeks: an aristocratic chieftain is only responsible for his own men and owes nothing to the soldiers led by other chieftains. The clash between the individualistic values of the nobility and the communal values of the city-state produced by this and similar Homeric usages shows that the social perspective adopted in the *Iliad* is a double one.

Notes

36. *Il.* 23. 536–8, 586–96, 884–97.

37. M.I. Finley, *The World of Odysseus* (2nd ed.), (Harmondsworth, 1978), 115.

38. See A.A. Long, "Morals and Values in Homer", *Journal of Hellenic Studies* 90 (1970), 123–26. On the values of Greek aristocracy see esp. W. Donlan, *The Aristocratic Ideal in Ancient Greece* (Wauconda, Illinois [repr. of Coronado Press, 1980], 1999).

39. *Il.* 9. 328–33.

40. *Il.* 9. 318–19; Ar. *Pol.* 1267a1–2.

41. M. Finkelberg, *"Timê* and *Aretê* in Homer", *Classical Quarterly* 48 (1998), 15–28.

42. *Il.* 11. 762–4, 16. 29–32, 18. 98–106.

Works by Homer

IN GREEK:

Opera. Ed. Demetrios Chalkokondyles, 1488.

Odysseia. Ed. Aldo Pio Manuzio, 1504.

Ilias et Odyssea. Ed. J. Micyllus, 1541.

Works. Ed. Jacobus Micyllus and Joachim Camerarius, 1541.

Ilias. Ed. Ioannis Crespini Atrebatii, 1559.

Ilias. Ed. Johann Guenther, 1563.

Ilias. Ed. Georgius Bishop, 1591.

Opera. Ed. Johannes Field, 1660.

Ilias. Ed. Johnanes Hayes, 1679.

Ilias. Ed. Thomas Day Seymour, 1695.

Opera. Ed. Samuel Clarke, 1740.

Works. Ed. Thomas Grenville, Richard Porson, et al., 1800.

Ilias et Odyssea. Ed. Richard Payne Knight, 1820.

Works. Ed. Wilhelm Dindorf, 1828.

Odyssey. Ed. Henry Hayman, 1882.

Odyssea. E. Arthur Ludwich, 1890.

Ilias. Ed. Dominicus Comparetti, 1901.

Opera. Ed. David B. Monro and Thomas W. Allen, 1912.

Odyssey. Ed. A.T. Murray, 1919.

Ilias et Odyssea. Ed. Eduardi Schwartz, 1924.

Odyssey. Ed. W.B. Stanford, 1948.

Odyssea. Ed. Helmut van Thiel, 1991.

TRANSLATED INTO ENGLISH:

The Whole Works of Homer. Trans. George Chapman, 1612.

Odyssey. Trans. John Ogilby, 1659.

Iliad. Trans. John Ogilby, 1660.

The Iliad and Odyssey of Homer. Trans. Thomas Hobbes, 1673.

The Iliad of Homer. Trans. Alexander Pope, 1720.

The Odyssey of Homer. Trans. Alexander Pope, William Broome, and Elijah Fenton, 1726.

The Iliad of Homer. Trans. James Macpherson, 1773.

The Iliad and Odyssey of Homer. Trans. William Cowper, 1791.

The Iliad of Homer. Trans. William Cullen Bryant, 1870.

The Odyssey of Homer. Trans. William Cullen Bryant, 1872.

The Odyssey of Homer. Trans. S.H. Butcher and Andrew Lang, 1879.

Iliad. Trans. Andrew Lang, Walter Leaf, and Ernest Myers, 1883.

The Odyssey of Homer. Trans. Willliam Morris, 1887.

The Odyssey of Homer. Trans. George Herbert Palmer, 1891.

The Odyssey of Homer. Trans. Samuel Butler, 1900.

The Iliad of Homer. Trans. Samuel Butler, 1898.

Iliad. Trans. A.T. Murray, 1924.

Odyssey. Trans. A.T. Murray, 1931.

The Odyssey of Homer. Trans. T.E. Lawrence, 1932.

Iliad. Trans. W.H.D. Rouse, 1937.

The Story of Odysseus. Trans. W.H.D. Rouse, 1942.

Iliad. Trans. Richmond Lattimore, 1951.

Odyssey. Trans. Robert Fitzgerald, 1961.

Odyssey. Trans. Richmond Lattimore, 1967.

Iliad. Trans. Robert Fitzgerald, 1974.

The *Iliad*. Trans. Martin Hammond, 1987.

The *Iliad*. Trans. Robert Fagles, 1990.

The *Iliad*. Trans. Ennis Rees, 1991.

The *Iliad*. Trans. Michael Pierce Reck, 1994.

The *Iliad*. Trans. Stanley Lombardo, 1997.

The *Iliad*. Trans. A.T. Murray (revised by William F. Wyatt), 1999.

Annotated Bibliography

Adkins, A.W.H. "Values, Goals, and Emotions in the *Iliad*." *Classical Philology* 77 (1982): 292–326.

Adkins concentrates on the values, emotions, goals, and behavior of some of the key characters in the Homeric poems. He explores how these relate to the thinking of the poet or poets of the pieces, the early Greek audiences, and readers in our own time. He concludes that Homeric values usually were admired uncritically by the Greeks and are "essentially the values of the modern nation-state." Adkins' *Merit and Responsibility*, published in 1960, also covers Homeric morality and much discussion resulted from it.

Dodds, E.R. *The Greeks and the Irrational*. Berkeley and Los Angeles: University of California Press, 1951.

Considered a pioneering and influential study, the work focuses on the value systems of Homeric and later Greek society. Dodds confronts the traditional view of Greek culture as a model of rationalism, using modern anthropology and psychology in his examination. The Greek view of madness and possession is explored, pressing the reader to reevaluate the modern vision of rationality.

Griffin, Jasper. *Homer on Life and Death*. Oxford: Clarendon Press, 1980.

Griffin focuses on Homer's view of what it means to be a hero, in life and death. He analyzes symbolic scenes, significant objects, and characterization. He also writes of Homer's use of gods and goddesses and how religion is presented in the work.

Kirk, G.S. *The* Iliad: *A Commentary*. Cambridge: Cambridge University Press, 1985–93, six volumes.

Kirk is the general editor of this multi-volume set of line-by-line commentary. Each volume contains introductory essays, and they are written by scholars J.B. Hainsworth, R. Janko,

M. Edwards, N. Richardson, and Kirk himself. Issues given notable attention are language, style, and thematic structure; also provided is social and cultural background.

Lesky, Albin, *A History of Greek Literature*, translated by James Willis and Cornelia de Heer, Thomas Y. Crowell Company, New York, 1966.

This is a survey of Greek literature, with many references to scholarly theories and a substantial bibliography. Specific to Homer are sections that cover the *Iliad*'s materials and composition, cultural levels in the poems, language and style, the gods' interactions with humans, and the epic cycle. Also addressed is epic poetry prior to Homer.

Albert Bates Lord. *Singer of Tales*, edited by S. Mitchell and G. Nagy. Cambridge, Mass.; London: Harvard University Press, 2000.

The best known of Lord's works, it has been controversial as well. An examination of oral literatures and traditions, the book presents studies of oral heroic poetry collected in the Balkans in the twentieth century and compares their authors' techniques to Homer's and some others. While similar work had been done earlier, Lord's presentation gained greater attention. Similarly, in this work Lord made more accessible and brought more attention to the work of Milman Parry. While originally published in 1960, *Singer*'s 2000 edition is updated and includes audio recordings of sections of the songs described in the text as well as visual material such as a film of one of the traditional singers.

MacCary, W. Thomas. *Childlike Achilles: Ontogeny and Phylogeny in the* Iliad. NY: Columbia University Press, 1982.

MacCary's review of the *Iliad* is psychoanalytic, and he places relevant Freudian concepts within the Western philosophical tradition. He views Snell and Fränkel's Hegelian reading as inadequate, contrasts it with humanist and structuralist readings of Whitman and Redfield, and thereby establishes his own perspective. He analyzes the text in terms of topics such as the value of women, the price of rape and murder, and narcissism.

Nagler, Michael N. *Spontaneity and Tradition: A Study in the Oral Art of Homer*. Berkeley, Los Angeles, and London: University of California Press, 1974.

Nagler agrees with Albert Lord's thesis that Homer was an oral poet who dictated the *Iliad* and *Odyssey* directly to a scribe under "conditions resembling a normal composition-in-performance." He discusses the traditional phrase, the motif sequence, and the "eternal return" in the *Iliad*'s plot structure.

Nagy, Gregory. *Homeric Responses*. Austin: University of Texas Press, 2003.

This work of Nagy's builds on his earlier books and responds to some of his critics. Here, in a series of essays, he further elaborates his theories on oral composition and the evolution of Homer's epics. He looks at such topics as the importance of performance and the interaction between audience and poet, and sees the "irreversible mistakes" and cross-references in the *Iliad* as evidence of artistic creativity.

Parry, Adam. "The Language of Achilles." *Transactions and Proceedings of the American Philological Association* 87 (1956).

This author examines the language of Achilles. He uses examples to show the uniformity of heroic language in the *Iliad*. But since Achilles' personality forces him outside the world of the typical hero, Parry explains, Homer must create unique speaking methods for him. Parry argues that Achilles' tragedy is his inability to escape the world that he has become alien to.

Parry, Milman. *The Making of Homeric Verse*, edited by Adam Parry. London: Oxford University Press, 1971.

Called "the father of modern Homeric scholarship," Milman Parry researched the use of formulaic language and greatly clarified the structure of oral epic. Many have commented on Homer's repeated use of the same descriptive phrases (fixed epithets) as appearing to be used to fill out a line's meter or to reinforce aspects of characters' personalities. Parry sees them as something much more and differentiates their significance when used to describe a particular character or when used to describe various characters.

Powell, B.B., and I. Morris, eds. *A New Companion to Homer.* Leiden, N.Y.: Brill Academic Publishers, 1995.

This text is composed of essays by thirty European and American scholars, covering the gamut of subjects on Homer, specifically from literary, cultural, and historical perspectives. They provide details on the current information and controversies enveloping Homeric studies.

Rutherford, R.B. *Homer.* Oxford: Oxford University Press, 1966.

Rutherford discusses history, myth, and poetry, the question of how the *Iliad* was composed and transmitted, and its reception during both ancient and modern times. He focuses on the structure, characterization, and themes of the work and the concept of war and the hero. Also addressed are the relationships and roles of gods and men, and Homer's presentation of choices and consequences.

Snell, Bruno. *The Discovery of the Mind: The Greek Origins of European Thought,* translated by T.G Rosenmeyer. Cambridge, Mass.: Harvard University Press, 1953.

Snell sees reversals of characters' thoughts as directly derived from the gods rather than as an indication of a divided self. He argues that the psychology portrayed in Homer's works can be perceived as a part of the path toward our understanding of human consciousness.

Stanley, Keith. *The Shield of Homer: Narrative Structure in the* Iliad. Princeton: Princeton University Press, 1993.

This text concentrates on the *Iliad*'s structure, discusses Homer's form, problems in the interpretation of Achilles' shield, the ring-composition in Homer's digressions, and oral theory. The author also gives careful attention to the structure of each of the books and discusses the reason for the book divisions. He provides a context for the work and explains how it may have changed from the original to what we read today.

Taplin, Oliver. *Homeric Soundings: The Shaping of the* Iliad. New York: Oxford University Press, 1995.

Taplin provides insights about structure and meaning, exploring the ethics of the epic in conjunction with its poetic and narrative techniques He emphasizes that the poem was meant to be heard and argues against those that say its complexities would not be recognized in this form. He argues that when the poem is divided into three parts, many connections become apparent, offering different perspectives on its language and theme, as well as its moral and political views.

Vivante, Paolo. *The Homeric Imagination*. Bloomington and London: Indiana University Press, 1970.

Vivante looks at the role of man and the gods in Homer, as well as at Homer's representation of nature, reality, time, and life. He advocates studying Homer's poems for how they appeal to our feelings and understanding, since in this way we will observe how true and imaginative his work is. Vivante believes that in regards to nature, Homer provides "a fresh feeling for what it is and what it means."

Willcock, M.M. "Homer, the Individual Poet." *Liverpool Classical Monthly* 3 (1978): 11–18.

While some have pointed to seeming inconsistencies in the *Iliad* to substantiate various views (such as that Homer is not the sole author), Willcock explains that often such lines are misread. Instead of inconsistencies, he shows that some of the lines referenced are actually the words of various characters (who say what fits their personality) and not the words or thoughts of the poet himself. Willcock is also author of *A Companion to the Iliad*, printed in 1976, an aid keyed to the Lattimore translation.

Contributors

Harold Bloom is Sterling Professor of the Humanities at Yale University. He is the author of over 20 books, including *Shelley's Mythmaking* (1959), *The Visionary Company* (1961), *Blake's Apocalypse* (1963), *Yeats* (1970), *A Map of Misreading* (1975), *Kabbalah and Criticism* (1975), *Agon: Toward a Theory of Revisionism* (1982), *The American Religion* (1992), *The Western Canon* (1994), and *Omens of Millennium: The Gnosis of Angels, Dreams, and Resurrection* (1996). *The Anxiety of Influence* (1973) sets forth Professor Bloom's provocative theory of the literary relationships between the great writers and their predecessors. His most recent books include *Shakespeare: The Invention of the Human* (1998), a 1998 National Book Award finalist, *How to Read and Why* (2000), *Genius: A Mosaic of One Hundred Exemplary Creative Minds* (2002), *Hamlet: Poem Unlimited* (2003), and *Where Shall Wisdom be Found* (2004). In 1999, Professor Bloom received the prestigious American Academy of Arts and Letters Gold Medal for Criticism, and in 2002 he received the Catalonia International Prize.

Pamela Loos has written and/or researched more than 35 volumes of literary criticism, covering authors such as Goethe and Cormac McCarthy. She also served as the project editor on *Women Memoirists*, vol. II.

C.M. Bowra was warden of Wadham College, Oxford. He published *Greek Lyric Poetry from Alcman to Simonides*, *Ancient Greek Literature*, and *From Virgil to Milton*.

Milman Parry was Associate Professor of Greek at Harvard University and author of *L'Epithète traditionnelle dans Homère* and *Les Formules et la métrique d'Homère*.

Erich Auerbach was Sterling Professor of Romance Languages at Yale University. He is the author of *Mimesis*, *Literary*

Language and Its Public in Late Latin Antiquity and in the Middle Ages and has written titles on Dante.

M.I. Finley has been a professor of ancient history at Cambridge University. He was elected a Fellow of the British Academy in 1971 and wrote several books, including *The Ancient Greeks*, *Aspects of Antiquity*, and *The Use and Abuse of History*. He also edited many volumes about ancient history.

Albin Lesky is the author of *History of Greek Literature*, *Greek Tragedy*, and *Greek Tragic Poetry*, all translated into English from German. He is also the author of several other titles in German.

Cedric H. Whitman was Eliot Professor of Greek at Harvard University. Among his books are *Sophocles: A Study of Heroic Humanism*; *Euripides and the Full Circle Myth*; and *The Heroic Paradox*.

G.S. Kirk had been Fellow of Trinity College and Regius Professor of Greek at the University of Cambridge. He has edited work of Homer's and is the author of *Myth* and co-author of *The Presocratic Philosophers*.

Jasper Griffin has been Professor of Classical Literature and Fellow of Balliol College, Oxford. He is the author of *Homer: The Odyssey* and *Latin Poets and Roman Life*. He has edited works of Homer and Virgil.

Seth L. Schein has been a professor of comparative literature at the University of California, Davis. He has published *Reading The* Odyssey: *Selected Interpretive Essays*.

Mark W. Edwards has been a professor of classics at Stanford University. He is the author of *Sound, Sense and Rhythm: Listening to Greek and Latin Poetry*. He has also edited Homer and others.

Bernard Knox has been Director Emeritus of Harvard's Center for Hellenic Studies in Washington, D.C. His many works include *Oedipus at Thebes* and *The Heroic Temper*, and he is the editor of *The Norton Book of Classical Literature*.

Joachim Latacz has been Professor of Greek at the University of Basel, Switzerland, has published *Homer: His Art and His World*, and is an editor and translator.

Albert Bates Lord was the author of *Singer of Tales* and *Epic Singers and Oral Tradition* and the editor of several titles.

Maureen Alden teaches classics at Queen's University of Belfast. She has authored *Homer Beside Himself* and a book on pre-Mycenaean and early Mycenaean graves.

Margalit Finkelberg has been Professor and Chair of Classics at Tel Aviv University. She is the author of *The Birth of Literary Fiction in Ancient Greece*, *The Descendants of Hellen*, and numerous articles on Greek language, literature, and civilization.

Acknowledgments

"The Characters" by C.M. Bowra. From *Tradition and Design in the* Iliad: pp. 209–10, 213–14. ©1930. Reprinted by permission of Oxford University Press.

"The Traditional Metaphor in Homer" by Milman Parry. From *Classical Philology* 28 (January–October, 1933): pp. 41–43. ©1933 by the University of Chicago Press. Reprinted by permission.

"Odysseus' Scar" by Erich Auerbach. From *Mimesis: The Representation of Reality in Western Literature*, translated by Willard R. Trask: pp. 17–18, 23. ©1953 by Princeton University Press, 1981 renewed Princeton University Press, 2003 paperback edition. Reprinted by permission of Princeton University Press.

"Morals and Values" by M.I. Finley. From *The World of Odysseus*: pp. 118–20. ©1954 by M.I. Finley. Reprinted by permission of Viking Penguin, a division of Penguin Group (USA) Inc.

"The *Iliad*: Materials and Composition" by Albin Lesky. From *A History of Greek Literature*, translated by James Willis and Cornelis de Heer: 31–32. ©1957/58 by A. Francke. Reprinted by permission of Hackett Publishing Company, Inc. All rights reserved.

"Homeric Character and the Tradition" by Cedric H. Whitman. From *Homer and the Heroic Tradition*: pp. 161–62, 163–64. ©1958 by the president and fellows of Harvard College. Reprinted by permission.

"The Plain Style Reconsidered" by G.S. Kirk. From *Homer and the Oral Tradition*: pp. 105–107. ©1976 by Cambridge University Press. Reprinted by permission of Cambridge University Press.

Index

powers of, 22, 56
Athena in *The Iliad*, 19, 23, 95
  help to the Achaeans, 22, 25, 27, 30–35, 37, 41–42, 54–60
  powers of, 22, 76
Auerbach, Eric
  on *The Iliad*, 25

B
"Battling for the Ships" (book thirteen), 44–45
Bible, 7
  heroes of, 8, 68–69
  The Iliad compared to, 24, 68–69
  New Testament, 24
  Odyssey compared to, 68
  Old Testament, 68–69
Briseis in *The Iliad*, 62
  grief, 65
  stealing of, 20, 25, 28, 38, 40, 53–54, 97, 101
Bronze Age, 12
Bryant, William Cullen, 13

C
"Champion Arms for Battle" (book nineteen), 53–54, 86
Chryseis in *The Iliad*
  war prize, 20, 24–25
Chryses in *The Iliad*, 20, 24–25

D
Danaans in *The Iliad*. *See* Achaeans; Argives; or Greeks
Dante, 68
Dardanians. *See* Trojans in *The Iliad*
"Death of Hector, The" (book twenty-two), 57–58, 86
Deïphobus in *The Iliad*, 20–21, 44–45, 57–58
"Diomedes Fights the Gods" (book five), 31–34
Diomedes in *The Iliad*, 19
  characteristics, 66, 72–73, 76

warrior, 16, 18, 20, 31–38, 40–42, 45, 59–61
Dolon in *The Iliad*, 65
  death, 41
  spy, 20, 41

E
"Embassy to Achilles, The" (book nine), 38–40, 84, 98–99
Eumelus in *The Iliad*
  chariot-driving, 16, 59–60, 100
Evans, Arthur
  excavation sites, 12

F
Fagles, Robert
  translation of *The Iliad*, 12, 24
fate theme
  in *The Iliad*, 15, 33, 40–41, 46–47, 50, 54, 56
Finley, Moses, 100
"Funeral Games for Patroclus" (book twenty-three), 58–61, 99

G
Glaucus in *The Iliad*, 20, 34, 43, 49–50
Gods and Goddesses in *The Iliad*
  Aphrodite, 19, 22–23, 29, 32–33, 46, 55–56, 89–90, 95
  Apollo, 20–23, 25, 33, 35, 41, 46–47, 49–51, 55–57, 59, 61, 65, 82
  Ares, 22–23, 31–34, 54, 56
  Artemis, 22–23, 56
  Athena, 19, 22–23, 25, 27, 30–35, 37, 41–42, 54–60, 76, 95
  Dione, 22
  Hades, 22–23
  Hebe, 22–23
  Hephaestus, 22–23, 52, 56, 86–87
  Hera, 22–23, 33–34, 37, 45–47, 54, 56, 89–90, 95
  Hermes, 23, 61–62
  Iris, 23, 46–47, 52

121